THE STRUGGLE TO BE FREE

THE STRUGGLE
TO BE FREE:
My Story and Your Story

By
WAYNE E. OATES

THE WESTMINSTER PRESS
Philadelphia

First edition

Published by The Westminster Press®
Philadelphia, Pennsylvania

PRINTED IN THE UNITED STATES OF AMERICA
9 8 7 6 5 4 3 2 1

Library of Congress Cataloging in Publication Data

Oates, Wayne Edward, 1917–
    The struggle to be free.

    1. Oates, Wayne Edward, 1917–   . 2. Baptists—
United States—Clergy—Biography. 3. Pastoral psychology
—United States—History—20th century. I. Title.
BX6495.O27A37 1983   286'.132'0924 [B]   83-5904
ISBN 0-664-24500-5 (pbk.)

In Memory of My Mother and Her Mother

LULA OATES
and
MARY JANE CAPELL

Contents

Acknowledgments

CONCERNING THE CONTENTS of this book, I want to acknowledge my debt to all those in my heritage who shaped my earliest years by their love and character. My mother, my grandmother, my sister, and my two brothers all had a hand in shaping the beginnings of my life. My father, whom I never really knew, had a positive symbolic influence on the kind of person I have become.

By far the most influential in my years after the age of thirteen have been my teachers and mentors. The following pages tell that story, but I acknowledge here that my teachers have enabled me to enter into the fruits of their labors and then celebrated achievement with me. To them I acknowledge my debt also.

This book is about the struggle to be free. Never before in my life have I enjoyed the kind of responsible freedom made possible for me by the faculty of the School of Medicine where I now work. Particularly responsible for this is Professor and Chairman John Schwab, M.D., and the faculty of the Department of Psychiatry and Behavioral Sciences. For their generosity and colleagueship, I acknowledge my deep gratitude.

I owe much gratitude to my colleague Henlee Barnette, and to Helen Poarch Barnette, for having read this manuscript and made very helpful suggestions. Likewise, I am indebted to

Andrew Lester for his suggestions upon having read these pages. I incorporated all of their very helpful comments.

My wife, Pauline Rhodes Oates, has lived most of these years with me as my loving comrade. She has read the manuscript and made specific suggestions and seen to it that the best wisdom has been used.

Most specifically, I acknowledge the indispensable help of Mrs. Jenni Khaliel, my research assistant. She has seen to it that I make the best sense possible in this and other books. Her commitment to excellence and to letter perfection has disciplined these pages. To her I acknowledge my sincere debt and appreciation.

The publication of this book marks thirty-two years of my work with Westminster Press, and particularly Dr. Paul Meacham as my guiding editor. I know that Paul Meacham's own inherent modesty would prompt him to want no acknowledgments. However, my own gratitude to him must have its way just this once. He opened a vast ecumenical audience to me in 1950; he developed with me a style, format, and substance for my writing that is uniquely my own but brought to its best level of utterance by his editorial wisdom. Therefore, I want here to acknowledge my debt as an author, my appreciation of him as my editor, and my gratitude to him and to God for his steadfast friendship.

W.E.O.

School of Medicine
University of Louisville
Louisville, Kentucky

Prologue

YOUR STRUGGLE to be free is different from mine. We are kinspersons in that we both struggle. Yet you may not perceive your life as a struggle in any sense of the word. You may be a child of destiny for whom doors simply opened to you in an ordered and anticipated manner. Even so, life was not that easy for many people whom you know and who are genuinely important to you. Thus I hope this book will speak to needs with which you are familiar and will not be read simply as a written account of an isolated and quaintly different person. I want a shared comradeship with you as my reader

For me, life has from the first been a struggle. From my earliest memory I have contended with adversaries of superior number and strength. I have offered obstinate resistance to forces of constraint and sought to escape from those forces that constricted my freedom. You ask: "Freedom to do what?" Freedom to decide my own destiny; freedom to choose my own direction; freedom to express my own thoughts; freedom to work in my own way; freedom to put into action what God has destined that I be and become. That is a vague answer. I hope to make it specific and clear in these pages.

In any event, the struggle has always been between the "from" and the "to"—freedom from one thing in order to devote myself to another thing. That struggle has been mine since my conception. Rebekah gave birth to twins, Esau and

Jacob. They struggled with each other in the womb before their births. I was not a twin. But the contending forces have always been within me as well as without, whether to "fit in" and become comfortable or to break out of the mold, the pattern, the role, the situation, the condition of life, into a yet undiscovered, unsought for, and unrealized realm of being. I have struggled against the former and opted for the latter.

You too have a longing to move from one condition to another more satisfying and deep. Let us join together in "the struggle to be free."

1
To Be Free from Poverty

As I BEGIN my story, I want you to think of me as "reporting" on my life and times as a living human document of struggle. Life without struggle is but dull habit. Life with struggle is often painful and sometimes perilous, but always adventurous. The writing that follows sometimes becomes introspective, and I sense you as my reader as *my* listener.

Sometimes I think private thoughts out loud, but I promise that as I come to the end of each chapter, I shall return to vigorous dialogue with you about your struggles *and* my struggles, as it were, with God's own messenger whom we will not let go until he has blessed us.

Scarcity and scantiness of food, clothing, and shelter trapped my family and me from my earliest memory. I am the youngest of four children. My next oldest sibling was a brother, Ned, six years older than I. Next to him was another brother, Frank, five years older than Ned. Next to Frank was my sister, Lois, five years older than he. We were all far enough apart in years to have a sort of world alone in which to grow up. We knew what it was to be cold, poorly clad, and hungry. We knew what it was to live in shabby, unheated, squalid housing.

I was born in Greenville, South Carolina, on June 24, 1917; and I write this in the year of my sixty-fifth birthday. My mother and father had begun their lives on farms in the hill country of Pickens County. They were among those sharecroppers who moved from small farms to the textile mills of South Carolina in the last two decades of the 1800s and the first two decades of the 1900s. Whole families were employed as families, including children above the age of ten. They were housed in "mill houses" with a common water pump in the streets. At the age of ten my mother started to work in the mills laying up strands of cotton for spinning machines.

I am not aware of how my father and mother met and married nor of what their life together was like. I know that my father became involved with another woman and left us for her within weeks after I was born. Yet I wondered if it were that simple. I lived with the private hope that he would return and we would have a father. I saw him only twice that I remember: once when I was four he came in a car and took me for a ride; then I saw him again when I was ten when he came by our house for a brief visit. I have often wondered if the increased responsibility of four children were not too much for him to manage. Yet he never returned home.

When I was seventeen I received a letter from my father asking me to come to live with him. He said he was going to Brazil to help start a cotton mill there. Would I go with him? I wrote him that I could not do this; my mother was ill and out of work and I must work to support us. A week later he died suddenly. That night I dreamed that he was being buried and I was being buried with him. Even then I knew that the "me" being buried was my dream that he would return and save us from the wretched poverty we suffered.

I took the responsibility of examining court records and getting witnesses to establish the legality of my mother's marriage and his fathering us as children. In that way the $1,000 insurance policy he left became the property of my mother. When all his bills were paid, each of us in the family received $75 apiece. This helped pay my tuition in my sophomore year in college. This, to my knowledge, was the one financial contribution of my father to me.

The end result of this abandonment by my father was that my mother, my sister, and my two brothers worked in the mills from my earliest years. All together they made less than $30 a week. By this time, a child could not go to work until he or she was fourteen. The custom was that a child usually went to school through the sixth grade, or the seventh at most, and then started to work. How would I miss it?

My grandmother (my mother's mother) was a widow. From before my birth she lived with us. She took care of me as a baby and as a preschool child. She had never been to school, but she had taught herself to read, spell, and write. She used the same methods to teach me to do so before I went to public school. She taught me very early to love words. She loved me with an undivided affection. I loved her. She was for all practical purposes my mother. Yet my own real mother was used up by running a set of looms in the mill. She went to work at seven in the morning and got off at six in the evening. I can remember running to meet her in the dark of the evening to walk back to our house with her holding her hand. When she got home she was exhausted. I never remember her in my earlier years as anything but a sad, worried, fatigued person. There was never enough money for the basic necessities of life. She was always in debt to the company store and to loan sharks who charged 20 percent on the dollar per week.

We were in bondage to poverty. There was no way out. From my earliest years, my mind paced back and forth in this cage of want. Food was at a premium. We lived on dried pinto beans, turnips and turnip greens, corn bread and molasses Except for the meat that was the fattest of pork sold in salty blocks at the company store and called "fatback," my later study of nutrition tells me that I had a basic maintenance diet, but I was ashamed of it then. Sometimes we were fortunate enough to have a cow that provided milk and butter, but not often. In the main, as my grandmother put it, we were doomed "to live out of a paper sack." To her this meant that we no longer had room for a garden and the farm produce she had enjoyed on the farm. Whatever we got we bought at the company store, and brought it home in a paper sack. And there was little money to buy it with, to speak frankly.

You would think I was an unhappy child. I was not. I knew I was loved, even by my brothers, who resented the attention I got, and especially by my sister, with whom I have even to this day had a tender and adoring comradeship. I also had the love and friendship of "mother-goodwives" of the neighborhoods wherever we moved. (We moved twenty-seven times before I finished high school.) I learned early that if I were at hand when they were churning milk and preparing lunch for the menfolks, I would get a chunk of corn bread and fresh butter. One of them even took me to church once, and yet I did not feel that my clothes were good enough for me to be there. Neither could I make sense out of the way the hymnbook was written. Church was not a way of life for my family. My mother, grandmother, and sister were devout women of faith in God. Only my sister attended church. For poor people, church is too often another luxury to which they have no sense of being entitled or belonging. They can think of a thousand excuses, but this lack of a sense of franchise, this absence of a sense of entitlement, is their unspoken reason. After all, except for "Holy Roller" cottage prayer meetings, it cost money to go to church.

Poverty as a System

Poverty is far more than simply not having money, goods, and luxuries. Poverty is a way of life which, when once learned, is very difficult to unlearn. Poverty is a system of distrust of authority. Poverty is a system of temporary alliance between men and women which results in children, but the men are unable to contribute to their support. Poverty is a value system that shapes people's group behavior and casts out the members who do not conform to an unspoken code. Poverty has a subculture language system that reinforces a sense of kinship. Let me explain each of these facets of the poverty system.

Poverty for us was an "us-against-them" system. In the case of sharecroppers, "them" was the landowner who rode around you while you worked, and rode *you* when crops were sold. To the cotton mill worker, "them" was the superintendent, the boss weaver, the boss spinner, the "second hand," etc. Too fiercely outspoken and independent ever to form a labor union, the textile workers existed in a poverty system that considered anybody wearing a white shirt and a tie as "them." In a sense, we were as much in bondage to our own passive-aggressive resentment of the "up and out" as we were to the low wages and bad housing, the bare subsistence diet, and our own down-and-out status in life. The very act of collaborating with a more affluent person in the community was interpreted as trying to get on the good side (although that is not exactly the way it was said) of the bosses, as "forgetting your raising," etc. To associate with educated persons such as teachers, local college professors, etc., was to be "too big for your britches," to think you were "better than anybody else." It was to invite ridicule, practical jokes, and being shoved around physically.

The poverty system, furthermore, was a woman-centered world. Men and women in poverty formed sexual liaisons that produced children, but the men exited when the care of children became too great a burden for them. This led to the dominance of women in the care of children. Usually, the grandmother, mother, and daughter took charge, divided the labor, and learned to survive without the man. Eric Wolf calls this the "matri-focal" unit and says that it appears among "economically depressed urban groups" (Eric Wolf, *Peasants*, p. 62; Prentice-Hall, 1966). This was the case in our family.

My father exited when I was born, leaving my care to my mother, grandmother, and sister. My sister became the mother of five children. Her husband was a World War I veteran who was both an alcoholic and a bootlegger during the Prohibition era. He was in jail when my sister's first child was born. Both of my brothers married, became the fathers of children—two sons in the case of one and two daughters in the case of the other. They both separated from their wives and left them to lead and care for their children. Each, like my father, died an early death. The isolation and loneliness of these men, my father and my two brothers, was great. My own care of them was cut off at my birth, in the case of my father, and later by my brothers' rejection of me as an educated person who—in their opinion —thought he was "better" than they. I did not give them money when they were broke. They perceived me as making bundles of money as a struggling college and seminary student. In fact, when they worked as weavers in the mills, they made *more* than I did after World War II when the Great Depression had lifted. I was in college and seminary during the Depression and the first part of World War II. We became strangers to each other. I did not feel that I could go home again. I avidly read the novels of Thomas Wolfe—that fellow Carolinian born sixty miles from where I was born, into a similar world.

My brothers loved me, but they could not stand the sight of me. My own shared stubbornness refused to permit me to be pushed around by them. When I reached the fullness of my height and weight, I was bigger than they were. They quit ridiculing me then and simply withdrew from me as much as possible. When I learned my oldest brother had died, I had not seen him for twelve years. Strangely, about a week or ten days before his death, he called me and asked me for a hundred dollars. I readily told him I would send it to him. I went to the bank and borrowed it and sent it to him. I had a sense of repetition of my father's death when I learned that he had died. When my younger brother died, I had not seen him in over five years. He was a veteran of World War II. He suffered from a disabling nephritic heart condition and was put on disability by Cannon Mills in Kannapolis, North Carolina. He became ill and went four times, my sister told me, to the Veterans Hospital in Salisbury, North Carolina, asking to be admitted. They refused him admission four times. After the fourth time, he went home and died alone. He did not contact me at all before his death, nor did I know he was seriously ill. These are the stories of three men in the system of poverty and oppression I have been describing. They lived lonely, isolated lives and died lonely, isolated deaths. For them, the world was against them.

Again, poverty is a *value* system. Poverty-level people have a deeply ingrained but unwritten code. First, people of poverty resist being told what we *have* to do. We respond: "All I have to do is take my last breath and die." This belief caused my mother to quit her job often. We moved often as a result. The more we moved, the less we had. Second, people of poverty can be divided into two groups in our attitudes toward work, those of us who insist on having *no* set hours for work in order to come and go as we please, and those of us who are easily regimented into shiftwork hours. The former tend to be the "dirty," unskilled laborers. The others are the "clean" poor who are skilled laborers and can command better pay. When a present-day textile worker reads what I am writing here, he or she will be angered. However, *that* person reads! My people, except for my grandmother and sister, never read. Also, that person is the more ambitious, less poverty ridden person who is probably a church member. My people were not church members. Furthermore, I am describing conditions in cotton mills in the 1910–1945 time span. People now tell me that things are different. I want to believe them. However, when my ninety-one-year-old mother died in 1972, she had a $1,000 company insurance policy with Cannon Mills for which she and my sister had paid more than triple its face value. There was no such thing as "paid up to 65" for that company. When I saw this I could feel again the same old rage at the oppression of the cotton-mill system. It was as if all the yesterdays were today again all of a sudden. Yes, I am willing to grant you that the cotton-mill system has changed. I will have to take your word for it and say that it does not change thousands of my yesterdays and make alive that which was laid waste by it.

Another value of persons who have lived in poverty is directness of speech. We don't beat the devil around the bush. Tact, courtesy, smooth talk are not valued very highly. It is an act of cowardice to say something behind a person's back that you have not first said to him or her. Such forthrightness forgoes

having secrets. Yet this leads to many, many broken relationships. To say many things bluntly does not weigh the hurt
that words can cause. Yet, when push comes to shove, the ethic
of the poverty-stricken is to tell it like it is. Hence, persons who
have moved up out of poverty regardless of wealth or education
tend to suffer a sense of betrayal when people say things about
us without saying them first to us. On the other hand, our
frankness, unless accompanied with gentle humor, can
irreversibly wound people who had no desire to be our
enemies. In short, we make a great many unnecessary enemies
with brutal honesty.

One more aspect of poverty as a system is its language
system. Four-letter vulgar words are not vulgarities to poverty
folk. They are the only language for the parts of the body, the
personal functions of the body, etc. Similarly, language is
learned by oral tradition and this supersedes schoolroom
language because it represents one's bond with parents and
siblings and grandparents. In a contest, schoolroom language
loses. To speak "proper talk" means a break with one's raising.
Yet to speak poverty speech in the classroom is to be a poor
student. My solution was to become "bilingual." I spoke
poverty-ese at home and used big words at school. When I
wanted to put down my brothers I would use big words at
home. Usually I got my face pushed in for my "damn proper
talk." Yet when the family needed a spokesman with outsiders I
did the talking. It's crazy, but for a while it worked.

This language system has always fascinated me. When I
studied the history of the English language at Wake Forest
College, I discovered that my grandmother's and mother's
speech was replete with obsolete Old English and Old French
words and phrases such as "holpen" rather than "help" and
"this-here" and "that-there" rather than "this" and "that"—
precise translations of *ceci* and *cela*. In this I found a clue to
liberation from my poverty system rather than total denial of its
strengths. To this day, I retain a Southern drawl, the graphic
figures of speech, the proverbial sayings, and the directness of

speech in the language of my daily work. The language of poverty is prepositional, not nominative. One is "up against it," not "frustrated"; one is "into something," not "involved"; one is "at the end of his rope," not "desperate"; etc. To this day, I am wounded deeply by people who tell everyone but me what they think is wrong with me. Given a chance, I would have tried to rectify, make restitution, and set things right.

The poverty system has enough freedom from self-discipline and responsibility to make the poor prefer their bonds to the struggle for freedom from poverty. As Rousseau said: "Slaves lose everything in their chains, even the desire of escaping from them; they love their servitude. . . . Force made the first slaves, and their cowardice perpetuated it" (*The Social Contract*, Book I, Sec. 3). Even our Declaration of Independence expresses the subtle cooperation of the oppressed with the oppressor: "Mankind are more disposed to suffer, while evils are sufferable, than to right themselves by abolishing the forms to which they are accustomed." Any effort to be free of poverty calls for a stubborn, gutsy struggle. It is uphill all the way.

Freedom from Poverty

Freedom from poverty came to me as freedom to change my part in the system I have just described. It started with a lively curiosity about the world of which I was a part. For example, violent death occurred all around me. Men fought with razor-sharp knives. I saw a man with his stomach cut open in a barbershop fight. I saw a man and woman who had been stabbed to death by an irate husband who found his wife having sex with this man. I went to the graveyard where they were buried. That was my introduction at the age of four to the fact that people die. Religion likewise was tempestuous as I learned when I chinned myself at the window and saw a healing session of Holy Rollers casting out evil spirits. These things I observed with a sort of "fly on the wall" clinical detachment, wondering what made those people be that way. Years later Harry Stack Sullivan named my lonely belonging "participant observation."

This detached enmeshment in what was happening came to focus when I was in the second grade. I was watching other children playing on the school playground. I noted that I not only could watch them. I could also watch my own mind watching them. That was the first revelation of my way to freedom: I deeply knew that I had a mind within my mind that was *more* than my mind. (Later I read Immanuel Kant in his *The Science of the Right* when he said: "Freedom . . . is an innate quality belonging to every man . . . in which he ought to be his own master by right." He called it "the internal mine and thine"—*meum et tuum internum.*) I was *able* to think; I was able to observe others in action and yet be free of them. I was able to observe my own mind in action and exercise control over my own thoughts. To me this was my first step to freedom from bondage to the system of poverty. I felt the stirrings of an early friendship with God in this gift of his providence.

Another experience triggered my struggle to be free. I learned in school that teachers were my friends, not my enemies. The public schools were led by teachers who were clean. The soap they used was sweet-smelling. It smelled different from the strong Octagon soap we used. They were filled with new thoughts. They wanted us not only to write, but to write beautiful handwriting. They were devout and let their faith in God be known by the way they believed in me. They taught me *correct* English. I began to see that they were never critical of my flat, incorrect grammar learned at home, but they simply had a better way. By the time I reached the sixth grade I was writing on my own. I wrote and illustrated a "book" entitled "Man and Nature," in which I pointed out that inventions such as the camera and the airplane were man's copies of nature —the human eye and the bird that could fly.

Today, in a day when the public school is bureaucratized, politicized, vandalized, and terrorized, I attribute my opportunity in the struggle to be free from poverty to the *public* schools and a long series of competent, affectionate, and well-informed public school teachers. They believed that effective identification of the student with the teacher is the conduit of learning. One teacher in particular in the fifth grade, Miss Tilman, gave me confidence in my own mental abilities by her inspiring belief in me. She is a liberator of my mind and spirit whom I cherish to this day.

Earlier on, two events gave central theological heart to my sense of freedom as a child of poverty. The streetcars in Greenville met at our front door to use a spur track to pass each other. As one particular motorman waited, he would talk with me, laugh with me, and show me how the streetcar worked. I admired him greatly. In the concrete operations of my mind, I decided that God had to be like this streetcar motorman. He was a strong God. He guided and controlled the world the way this man did the streetcar. He shows us how the world works. He *laughs!* He likes *me*. We're friends. No religious teachers taught me this. I decided it for myself.

Another event occurred when I sat one day on the porch of a neighbor woman, watching her string beans for lunch. She told me: "You are not supposed to live your life like the rest of us have had to live ours. God has a purpose for you. You must find it." Her name was Mrs. Ingle. The sun was warm that day, but not too hot. The clickety-clack of looms and the roar of spinning frames gave sound and substance to what she said. I have never forgotten her or what she said. I took it to heart. I believed it.

Providence goes ahead of us, and Providence went ahead of me. The eighth grade was the countdown year. I loved school, loved learning, and loved exploration of a new world. The only thing to this point that had made school a terror to me was having to change schools. Being shifted from schools was always a time of bereavement for me. It seemed unimportant to my family, but it was a major crisis for me. Yet, the eighth grade was slated to be my last year of school because I would be fourteen after that year. Then I was to quit school and go to work.

I had found in school the avenue of my freedom from the

grinding poverty, ugliness, filth, and brutality I saw happening around me. I sensed that learning words would give me power for the struggle to be free. School—education—would be my avenue to the larger world of mankind where I could meet and learn from all kinds of people. But the countdown of my last year ticked away. Then something unheard of happened.

On Tuesday before Thanksgiving, 1930, the principal of the school came to the door of my class in civics taught by Mrs. Geiger. He asked for me. He took me to his office where he, Mr. Castle, Mr. Reams, the school coach, and Mrs. Mims, my geometry teacher, were gathered. They told me that United States Senator Ellison D. Smith had asked them to select a cotton-mill boy to be appointed by him as a page in the Senate. Would I like to be the person? After they explained the job to me, I told them I would do it because it meant I could keep on going to school and work, too.

Then they took me to the mill to see my mother and get her permission. She said calmly: "If Wayne thinks he can do it, he can do it." I have held this comment to me as her permission to go, yes, but more than that. I *could* do what I decided I could do. With those words of hers plans went into effect and six days later I was in Washington, D.C., after a long train ride, ready to go to work as a page in the Senate among a group of twenty other pages, all of whom had come from the most privileged homes in America.

I stayed there up to the last three months of my four years in high school. It was the decisive opportunity that set me free from the tyranny of a poverty system. For the first time I had enough food; for the first time I wore a suit of clothes, shirt and tie; for the first time I earned money for myself. But I was homesick, lonely, scared, and overwhelmed by my surroundings.

God's Action

Providence—the foreseeing power and action of God—made itself known to me in these dramatic events. I saw my way to freedom from the poverty system clearly for the first time. I felt that I had been delivered. Yet it was my challenge to discipline. Never again did I feel that I didn't have a chance. Was it an accident? Did I just happen to be in the right place at the right time? Why was I delivered and my brothers left in the system that finally ground the life out of them? Why was I a chosen and favored one when dozens of my classmates dropped out of school and became a part of the poverty system? Why is it now, when I consider the massive complexities of the burdens of my professional colleagues, my students, our patients, that I often think that running a set of looms might give one more peace and tranquillity?

I know none of the answers to these questions. I know that they follow me daily and prompt in me gratitude and mission, not complacency. Nor do I feel specially favored of God as over against my confreres in Parker High School in Greenville. More often I feel that they are the norm and I am the oddball, the strange one, the lonely one. One thing I know is that God intends that you and I consecrate our intelligence to its maximum growth through using it. Education became my God-given path to freedom. God does not intend that human intelligence be snuffed out by hunger, grinding poverty, and a squalid lack of care and discipline. I know this: that once we have won the struggle to be free of poverty, God intends that we have a burning sense of social justice that is dedicated to enabling others in that same struggle. I know that it is in the exercise of that sense of injustice that we find fellowship with him of whom it is recorded:

> And there was given to him the book of the prophet Isaiah. He opened the book and found the place where it was written,
>> "The Spirit of the Lord is upon me,
>> because he has anointed me to preach good news
>>   to the poor.
>> He has sent me to proclaim release to the captives
>> and recovering of sight to the blind,
>> to set at liberty those who are oppressed,
>> to proclaim the acceptable year of the Lord."

And he closed the book, and gave it back to the attendant, and sat down; and the eyes of all in the synagogue were fixed on him. And he began to say to them, "Today this scripture has been fulfilled in your hearing." (Luke 4:17-21)

A Common Theme

A persistent motif, a common theme, runs through your struggle and my struggle to be free of poverty. Words were powerful and set me free; they do not cost you a penny; they have the power to set you free. To have no language but a cry is to be an infant in the night, not to know what people mean. To have no language but the language of poverty is to ask to be bound to that system. You and I can break out into words and grow. To break out of the dialect of the poor is to struggle to be free. Yet not to engage in this struggle is to become accustomed to our bonds and shackles, even to the point of *preferring* them.

The uniqueness of your and my humanness lies in our capacity for words. Words became the Word when God chose to reveal himself fully in the flesh. The Word was made flesh and we beheld his glory, as of the only begotten of the Father, full of grace and truth.

The Blessing of Poverty: An Invitation to Dialogue

God never intends that you and I or our neighbors starve. Jesus fed the multitude with bread. The blight of malnutrition snuffs out the intelligence of a person as wind blows out a candle. You may have felt abject poverty, but it was not the intention of God. Yet you and I *were* poor. The blessing that poverty brought us is evident in the skills it taught us—the capacity for direct speech with each other; the capacity to remember when things were rougher than they are now; the powerful initiative that poverty generated in you and me; the sense of gratitude for the simple pleasures of life, the sense of their being luxuries and not inalienable rights. Yes, if you were poor, these are your legacies as they are mine. God has made all our adversities to turn out to his glory.

These are not the end of the blessings of poverty. Jesus said: "Blessed are you poor, for yours is the kingdom of God" (Luke 6:20). The poor person travels light. When Jesus commissioned the Twelve, he said: "Take no gold, nor silver, nor copper in your belts, no bag for your journey, nor two tunics, nor sandals, nor a staff." They were to forage upon the land, to survive on their relationships to those whom they met. He did *not* say that they were to starve. In the next breath, he said: "For the laborer deserves his food" (Matt. 10:9). This was *work* to which he assigned them and they were to be fed by those whom they served.

Not only were they to work; they were also to rest. You and I were never intended to work until fatigue blights our spirits and shatters our bodies, as was the case of my mother. For it was Jesus who said: "Come to me, all who labor and are heavy laden, and I will give you rest." In your and my pell-mell dash away from poverty, success and material symbols of affluence may erase the outward appearance of poverty. But our work addiction may rob us of the blessing of rest God intended for us in creation and Jesus promised us in redemption.

Paradoxically enough, Jesus *recommends* poverty as an antidote to greed and covetousness in some instances. He told the man who "had great possessions": "Go, sell what you have, and give to the poor, and you will have treasure in heaven; and come, follow me" (Mark 10:21). The man had forgotten the Tenth Commandment in his search for eternal life. Jesus told him that he needed to identify himself with the poor.

Have you ever wondered whether this man *earned* all his possessions or whether he *inherited* them? Let us suppose he had earned them. If so, he had "forgotten his raising." He had separated himself from the poor. Maybe he felt that anybody can "make a success of himself" if he or she tries. Maybe as a result he was contemptuous of the lazy, the shiftless, the "bums" he saw around him. Yet if the poor inherit the Kingdom of God, you and I are only very temporary stewards of what we possess. The ultimate curse of our possessions would be our assumption that we made them ours without God's help. The ultimate blessing would be an eager sense of gratitude for God's deliverance of us from hunger that makes us generous toward others who are struggling with poverty.

Your great blessing and my great blessing from the struggle to be free from poverty is our mission to see to it that these are ministered to through the fruits of our struggle.

2
To Be Free
from a Feeling of Inferiority

THE STRUGGLE with poverty is the struggle to survive—the struggle for food and clothing, the struggle with creditors, the struggle for the time to go to school, the struggle for a way out of the system that poverty both creates and symbolizes. Yet finding enough food and clothing and providentially being delivered from a self-perpetuating poverty system simply changes the struggle to another battleground

Poverty leaves you with wounds to your self-esteem. Your sense of self-worth is hobbled by a sense of shame and feelings of inferiority. These cannot be dealt with through better food, clothing, and surroundings. For me, at least, the struggle to be free from a feeling of inferiority has demanded that I affirm the strengths of my heritage without letting its limitations chain my spirit.

My earliest feeling of inferiority came just when Erik Erikson said it would—in the first years of school. For me it was a struggle to see whether high achievement as a student would win out over the fact that often my lunch was a cold biscuit with fatback in it while other children paid for lunch in the school lunchroom. Yet even making excellent grades was hindered by the hunger pangs that made a young boy have headaches late in the morning.

The feeling of shame came also when basketball and football games required money to buy a ticket. To be busy with a history, civics, English, or math project at game time was a compensatory explanation to other children, but the very busyness with these studies was a lonely venture.

Yet as long as I was in school where I was, enough other children were in similar circumstances that I did not feel vastly different from my peers. The irony came when I went to Washington, D.C., as a page in the Senate. Food, clothing, and shelter were plentiful. However, psychological and social collisions with feelings of shame and inferiority swept over me all the more. A few examples will make clear what I mean.

When I was a page, I lived in a boardinghouse that furnished room and two meals a day for $60 of the $150 a month I was paid. The food was better than anything I had ever known. They even served dessert at the evening meal. It took me a week of waiting for dessert after breakfast to figure out without asking someone that they just did not serve dessert for breakfast! To others this was simple assumption. To me it was total discovery. I just quit waiting for dessert in the morning.

Then again, at all meals there were different spoons and forks for each course in the meal. When we had fish I knew of only one way to separate the bones—with my fingers. I did not know what a napkin was for. Up to this time my shirt or coat sleeve served as napkin, handkerchief, and bandage. I shall never forget a beautiful older woman, Mrs. McKenzie, the secretary to Senator Heflin of Alabama. She asked me to sit by her at the table. She quietly and inconspicuously (that is, with no big to-do about it) showed me what genteel table manners are, how to maneuver my way through a somewhat formal meal. She was a beautiful woman of about fifty years of age, with strikingly pretty silver-gray hair and a gentle sense of humor. I was so grateful to her that the only way I could say "thank you" was with awed looks of worshipfulness in her direction. She unshackled me from my sense of ignorance, shame, and inferiority. She helped me in my struggle to be free with all kinds of people. She also gave me an incarnate picture of what a regal lady is like.

The struggle with inferiority feelings was at an all-time high, though, in relation to the other twenty pages on the Senate floor. I could do the complex work with ease: learning the names, faces, patterns of daily ritual, coats hats, canes, food and drink preferences, etc., of each of the ninety-six senators; keeping a file of new bills and resolutions introduced each day, a file of legislation returned from committee, and a file of legislation passed or rejected; knowing the office staffs of each senator; knowing how to identify a lobbyist and how to avoid becoming his messenger boy; being punctual, prompt, and swift in response to personal assignments from senators. These things I knew quickly how to do. I felt very competent in performing my job.

However, all the other pages were from privileged homes. They were sons of career government officials, grandsons of senators, sons of wealthy patrons of senators, etc. Yet behaviorally they were less well disciplined than my school-mates back home. They made fun of my speech, my cotton-mill background, my social shyness, and my personal appearance. They quickly noted that I had a body odor, dental problems, bad breath, and strange speech patterns. For the first year I was tormented, hazed, ridiculed, and beat up on by these people. I sought to make personal friends with them one by one to no avail. Consequently, my time off from work was spent in isolation from these persons. I was alone. That was it.

The void was filled in several ways. I went to night school at Hines Junior High School and took English, math, and typing. I learned touch-typing quite well, a skill I later used for many years when I had no secretary to prepare manuscripts for me.

Furthermore, I found that older persons at my boarding place invited me to go with them to art museums, the Smithsonian Institution, the Library of Congress, and the Folger Shakespeare Library. This created a habit and I then went alone to an unending number of repositories of art, science, literature, and American history in Washington. Whereas my obvious cultural deficiencies prompted ridicule of me by my fellow pages, it created concern and helpfulness in people older than I was. The awareness of this realm of culture was a galaxy of new worlds for my thinking. Music and companionship entered my world in free concerts by the Army, Navy, and Marine Corps bands held in the spring, summer, and fall on the steps of the Capitol. Young boys could meet young girls here in a well-disciplined setting. It cost no money because it was practice for the bands and free music for us. Conversation with girls from all over the country who were tourists was easy and appropriate. I can recall being the unofficial "guide" of several tourist sight-seeing families. They usually had a daughter who introduced me to her family. As I told them good-by, often the father paid me for my services as a guide. I think the love of good music was formed in my mind at these concerts. Even today I am refreshed in spirit and made free of inferior feelings to hear one of the military bands in concert on National Public Radio.

Another series of events aided me in my struggle to be free from feelings of inferiority. The Democratic pages were under the supervision of Mr. Leslie Biffle, a quiet and serious man. He was a stern disciplinarian, but an intensely fair person. He took my uncouth lack of culture far more seriously than Professor Higgins did Eliza Doolittle's in *My Fair Lady*. He taught me to bathe regularly and do away with body odor. He "diagnosed" my bad breath as a dental problem and sent me to Army dentists at Walter Reed Hospital. They removed remainders of my "baby teeth," filled cavities, and crowned a broken front tooth. Mr. Biffle demanded of all of us clean shirts, ties, cleaned and pressed suits, and shining shoes. We stood in line for inspection every morning.

But Mr. Biffle did more for me. Every time I made a grammatical error he corrected it on the spot. Every time he used a technical word he explained its meaning. When the Senate was in session, he urged me to listen closely to the speeches. When a new word appeared, he would hand me a vest-pocket dictionary he carried and expected me to look the word up and learn its spelling. It became a vocabulary game for us. Here again I found learning the English language well supplied me with the power to loosen the bonds of inferiority His patience with me was awesome. I see him as an early mentor who filled an aching void for a strong father figure. He cared enough to discipline me with language, manners, and personal hygiene rather than with petty rules. This newfound increase in confidence, self-worth, and personal dignity created a wide gap between my home environment and me. I was enriched by Mr. Biffle's discipline and the boardinghouse adults' tender comradeship with me as a young boy. I crossed a Rubicon of self-worth. There was never to be again a turning back—no matter what happened. I could hold my head high and not be ashamed.

During my second year as a page, my confidence in myself had grown. I was disillusioned with my peers. None of them, I felt, wanted me for a personal friend. Yet I was resolved that I had taken all the ridicule, abuse, and intimidation I intended to take. If they did not like me, they had another choice: to fear me. Consequently, I underwent a change of personality. I never again would be the shy, frightened, and pleading little boy that first came to Washington. I had learned to use my fists in fights with my brothers and in the streets and alleys of the cotton-mill village. I had expected the other pages to be gentlemen. They had forfeited that option. Therefore, I systematically used the next year to do two things—to be a friend to new pages and to give each of my old verbal tormentors a sound physical beating. In the last of these fights, my opponent fell on my right arm and it broke in the elbow. I carry a bent right arm that is an inch shorter than my left as a symbol of my decision never to be put down by anyone or to grovel in fear before anyone again, God being my helper.

Of course, Alfred Adler and Ralph Waldo Emerson before him would call this "compensation." I agree with them. I do think that the aggressive life-style of my ensuing years is a compensatory result of the feeling of inferiority. Yet I prefer intentional compensation with competent achievement to shriveling and shrinking self-depreciation, timidity, and fear of failure.

My aggressiveness came to Mr. Biffle's attention with my trip to the orthopedist's with a broken arm. That was the spring of 1932. It effectively ended my fistfighting days. Another demand on my nature lifted the aggressions to another arena. Senator Smith was running for reelection that summer. I was expected to do my part to help get him elected. We all rendezvoused in Columbia, South Carolina. I was to be an "ear" at company stores, at mill gates at shift change, in boardinghouses, and in door-to-door canvassing. My newfound chutzpah, brass, nerve, or initiative had a broad proving ground as I debated politics for Senator Smith with mill hands from Columbia west to Pickens, Travelers Rest, and Inman, South Carolina. I was answerable each week when I reported to the newspaper editors and Mr. Charles Jackson, Senator Smith's campaign manager.

Ellison D. Smith was no friend of Franklin Roosevelt. Smith was a professed champion of the cotton farmer, and a segregationist. It was intriguing to me to learn how power and influence are used, sometimes with great magnanimity of spirit, but at others with sheer cynicism on ethical issues. I learned that one of the first laws of politics is magnanimity when dealing with a helpless opponent. Voters rally around the underdog your lack of magnanimity creates. I learned that the underdog position is to be desired rather than the shoo-in position. Americans, anyhow, are instinctively for the underdog.

The cynical use of the race issue appalled me—appealing publicly to the paternalistic "care" of the "darky" and at the same time releasing rumors about the opponents' aiding and abetting the "kneegrow" (Negro) or "Nigra" (never quite "nigger") to enter a state university. In 1932 that was the way it was. Some changes have been made. Thank God! I learned the rudiments of psychological warfare through the deliberate use of rumor.

During this long hot summer, I sharpened the aggressive edge of my being through political debate. I had my first experiences as a public speaker at political rallies. It scared me and spurred me toward becoming an effective public speaker. From then on I grabbed every opportunity to develop my skills as a debater, a lecturer, a persuader. At last I found my true and trusted tool to replace fistfighting as a means of expressing my newfound aggressiveness. The use of the spoken word in a polished and dramatic style all my own would become in addition to my way of continuing to struggle with poverty also my way of struggling to be free of a crippling sense of inferiority. Mr. Biffle's continued discipline of my speech, my vocabulary, and my manners strengthened this resolve daily. The exact nature of the *content* of what I would say in public speech was nebulous in my mind. But as a ninth-grader, it seemed to me that being a lawyer would be the thing. The courtroom and politics would be the arena. This increased as a resolve of mine from that time until the beginning of my sophomore year in college, five years later.

The seeds of disenchantment with the political arena were sown during the 1932 reelection campaign. I once again became the observer more than the participant. I became aware that my appointment as a page boy from the cotton-mill district, as a boy who had no father, and as one who would not have had a chance to go to school, was a political move of value to a senator who was short of votes among textile workers. They scratched my back and I scratched theirs—at best something just short of jungle morality. However, it was better to eat and have a chance to go to school than to work fifty to sixty hours a week sweeping floors, emptying bobbin cans, and filling bobbin batteries on looms for five to six dollars a week. Even so, I was disenchanted by seeing members of the families of senators on government payrolls while patronage appointees worked all day and at night to do the work of the family members who were not even in Washington. I was disenchanted by seeing the starving, half-naked veterans of World

War I camped out on the Capitol grounds. Later they were dispersed by turning on the sprinkler system and bringing in Douglas MacArthur's troops. They were in poverty too.

Nevertheless, the senator won the race for reelection. He began a fifth term as Senator "Cotton Ed" Smith from South Carolina. I returned to Washington in 1932 with him. I had already seen Herbert Hoover sadly leave the White House. I heard Franklin Roosevelt make his "we have nothing to fear but fear itself" inaugural speech. Slightly above this noise of solemn assemblies I kept hearing about a German politician named Adolf Hitler and that the youth of Germany were gathering around him. These vectors of national and international politics were of the utmost concern to me as a tenth-grader. Little wonder, then, that when I visited back at home with former schoolmates, I was to them a real smart aleck who thought he was "better than anybody else." To my brothers, I was becoming increasingly a stranger. My mother was perplexed and wanted me to send my paycheck home to her, except for my barest necessities. My brothers were on relief jobs. The mills were laying off people by the thousands. Yet she managed to keep her job. She did not know how little I had left after I paid for room, board, laundry, carfare, books, etc. When I was at home I made no money. What a mess! All this made my spirit a battleground between an emerging self-confidence and verbal ability, on the one hand, and a family hopelessly trapped in the poverty system, on the other. This aggravated my feelings of inferiority.

Respectability itself can be a sort of bondage to people who are "born with a silver spoon in their mouth." To a person born into poverty, respectability is a hard-earned triumph over being inferior, as well as over seeing oneself, and being seen by others, as inferior. The struggle for respectability among other people in the poverty areas where my family lived often took on a religious quality. They started going to church. I came to this homegrown variety of freedom from a feeling of inferiority by going to church with a girl I met while home from Washington the summer of 1932, the campaign summer. I became interested not only in her but also in the activities of a youth group. There were chances to make speeches in these groups. I eagerly took these chances. I was even called on to pray. This I did. Then one young person asked our leader, a ministerial student from Furman University, whether God would hear my prayer inasmuch as I was not a baptized Christian. He replied: "No. His prayers didn't get any higher than the ceiling because he is not baptized."

This did not anger me as much as it intrigued me. I had been praying privately and being very aware of the Presence of God since I was four. This had little to do with going to church or praying in public. It had no Biblical teachings wrapped around it. It was real, private, and had kept me steady in the intense loneliness of two years in Washington where I worked as a page by day and went to school by night. My relationship to God was that I was sure I had a destiny, a purpose, a calling to fulfill. I was sure that God was with me and guiding me. I knew little or nothing about Jesus of Nazareth. God, though, was very personally active in my life. I suppose in Biblical terms, which I learned much later, I was like Cornelius, who was said to be "a devout man who feared God . . . and prayed constantly to God" (Acts 10:1-2).

Nevertheless, it was not long after this that the wife of the pastor of that church spoke to me and asked me if I would like to be a Christian. I told her yes, I would. That evening I went forward and asked to be accepted as a candidate for baptism upon a profession of my faith in Christ. I was baptized just as I had turned sixteen.

To me this meant that I had as much right as anybody else to pray. It meant that I felt responsible to God from then on for my behavior and my sense of purpose in my work. Yet, it was a remarkably *contentless* experience. I did not get any specific instructions as to who Jesus Christ is, as to *what* I had agreed to be and become, beyond simply being a "good person," a thing I had been striving for all along. The pastor asked me to come to see him. The one topic we discussed was that I was a page in the Senate and earned money. I was instructed to give a tithe of this to support the church. This I did not do. I felt very misunderstood by him—although further maturity makes me understand that he too was at the edge of poverty. Yet I was courteous to him and simply listened to him. He showed no interest in my family, the nature of my work, or anything of the sort. He did not know that I did not make money when I was not in Washington and when Congress was not in session. He gave me no instructions about what redemption in Christ was all about. This is what I mean by *contentlessness*. I had faith, but not according to knowledge.

More than this—I had no strong Christian man in my life who would be my mentor, teacher in the faith, and hero to follow. The pastor was a deprived man too. His wife was a kind, energetic, and considerate person. Her devotion to me, along with that of my girl friend, kept me actively attending the church. Then, too, I had the assurance that my prayers got higher than the ceiling. Another source of inferiority had been removed.

The more profound experience of Christian redemption came to me later. In rapid succession many events took place. I continued my work as a page until the spring of 1933. I reached my sixteenth birthday and was beyond eligibility as a page. I was "retired" as a page and given odd jobs as an elevator operator in the Senate Office Building, a Capitol guardsman, etc. I was offered an opportunity to complete high school and take an appointment to the United States Naval Academy. I was overwhelmed with uneasiness. I did not want to do any of these things.

One Sunday evening during the early winter I slipped into a Methodist church service and prayed quietly during a worship service as to the direction of my life. The distinct impression and sense of resolve came to me that I should return to my home in Greenville and finish high school with my class. I asked Senator Smith for letters of recommendation to federal offices in Greenville for a job. I returned home and took a job in the Emergency Relief Administration as a clerk writing grocery orders for families out of work. They stood in endless lines as they waited for sheets of paper telling them how much meat, potatoes, canned vegetables, flour, etc., they could get from distribution warehouses down the street. I wrote one every week for my own family.

It was a rude awakening to the Great Depression. None of these people had a history of being on government welfare before. The reason was simple: there had never been such a thing before. Work was provided, made, simulated, and imagined for them to do. If a person did not work, he or she got no food. People built roads; they planted trees; they built parks; they built government buildings; they chopped firewood. Much of it was make-work with little purpose.

In the meantime, I studied my lessons at night and passed my courses by taking tests with the rest of my class. I made good grades. I finished high school at Parker High School in May 1934.

In August 1934, a general strike hit the cotton mills in Greenville. People were fired for participating in it. The National Guard, machine guns and all, restored law and order. I got a job hauling cloth to the "cloth room" in Monaghan Mills as a result of the firings. It was a night-shift job. I stood it for seven months and went to Kannapolis, North Carolina, to live with my sister and her family while I learned to weave on huge Jacquard looms. I learned quickly and was given a set of six massive looms to run, weaving brocade bedspreads and sheets. For nineteen months I was what everyone in my family had been—a weaver. The pay was fifty cents an hour. If I made faulty cloth, I was "docked," i.e., money was taken from my paycheck as a penalty. Perfection was demanded; imperfection was punished.

The job was overwhelming. The massive noise, the lint-filled air, the intolerably sticky heat (even in winter), the crude humor, brutality, and lack of learning of other workers appalled me. My vocabulary, my speech carefully disciplined by Mr. Biffle, though, stayed just as it was. Each day that I worked, I prayed for a chance to get out of there and go to college. I vowed to do this, come hell or high water. This was no condemnation of the work itself, because I came to know, respect, and appreciate many of my co-workers in the mills. I learned from them how important a church can be in your life. I became a regular church attender at this time. My Christian faith began to take on substantive content. I read closely small "study course" books for lay people and attended groups where we discussed them. I became devoted to one Sunday school teacher, Zettie Walters, whose consistent and happy Christian life was very convincing to me. He was constantly prodding young men in his class to get an education. I was urged by him to do so. I met a YMCA group leader, B. G. Henry, an elementary school principal, who demanded a decision of me about going to college. He did more. He took me in his car to Mars Hill College, near Asheville, North Carolina, and introduced me to President R. L. Moore, and we made plans for me to enter there in the fall of 1936.

I saved $125 to enter school and was assured "work grants" at ten cents an hour to cover the rest of my expenses. Thus, I left the mills again. I have always been grateful that I worked for two years amid the lint-filled air, the noise, and the demands for perfection of work. It has made me, a weaver, all the more grateful for my mother, my sister, and my brothers in their care of me when I was small, helpless, and at the mercy of the world. At great cost to themselves, they provided many years of food, shelter, affection, and protection for me. I was a "Wayne-come-lately" to their scene, but I was never neglected, farmed out to some social agency, or treated as inferior. To the contrary, they seemed to feel that they had a bright person on their hands and put up with my penchant for school, books, big words, and farfetched dreams of things like public speaking, college, and—later on—reading the Bible. Yet from the time I left home to go to Washington at the age of thirteen, they let me fend for myself. As my mother put it: "You have got sense enough to get out of anything you get into if you don't want to stay in it." For a long time this comment has been the story of my life in a proverb.

Mars Hill College was located in an emerald ring of mountains. Low-lying clouds clustered at the tops of the mountains early in the mornings. The hills were alive with the idealism of the small junior college. The overwhelming majority of students were from culturally deprived and economically depressed homes when I was there. We ate simple but abundant food that we cooked in a common kitchen. We did all the cleaning and maintenance, and much of the landscaping, construction, and road-building for the college. We earned money provided by the National Youth Administration and by donations from friends of the college.

Yet there were also well-to-do students. Their parents had jobs! They were not in the majority, but they had had better backgrounds and were often better students.

I was three years older than most of the students and I was far more experienced at work and had more political acumen. My years as a page, though kept a closely guarded secret by me, paid off on initial placement exams in English, history, sociology, and geography. Very early I took the lead in English classes. By the second semester, I was a student assistant and understudy of Dr. Ella Pierce, who had a Ph.D. in English from Columbia University and had chosen to devote her life to young people at Mars Hill. She was as exacting in English grammar, spelling, punctuation, and elements of style in writing as Mr. Biffle had been. During two years of intense supervision by her, I resolved to be a writer at whatever I did for a living. That resolve never weakened but has always become more intense as I have striven to write.

At Mars Hill I knew *no* inferiority. Here I was decidedly acceptable to myself and respected by others. One chain of bondage to inferior feelings was effectively broken by my pen and typewriter. Hence, my typewriter—especially—has taken on an intense symbolism for me. For forty-two years I typed all my first drafts. Only in the last four years have I been blessed with a full-time research assistant, Mrs. Jenni Khaliel, to put my first drafts into typewritten form.

A second force of freedom from inferiority came to me at Mars Hill. The whole place vibrated with intense activity in speech, debating, drama, and oratory. We had a regular pyrotechnic display of closely refereed competition in these skills. These "indoor sports" outclassed athletic events for first place. After all, they did not call for expensive equipment—just a room and an audience. In good weather, we had outdoor dramas in an amphitheater we had built with our own labor.

Here again I shook myself free of a lack of confidence and a feeling of inferiority in developing my own style of public speaking. I learned the potent force of persuasive speech. It was a world of shared strength with fellow debating team members, with oratorical and declamation teams, etc. Once again, I progressed in the struggle to be free through the spoken word. The graphic speech my grandmother taught me, the exact speech Mr. Biffle taught me, and the art of public speech my speech teachers and debate coaches taught me at Mars Hill all benevolently inspired me to think more confidently of myself as a human being. I was on the verge of learning the Source of this power.

At Mars Hill mental discipline and spiritual discipline were one piece of cloth. For the first time I took serious course work in the Old and New Testaments. Under the weekly preaching of William L. Lynch, the pastor of Mars Hill Baptist Church, I learned the central message of the New Testament, particularly. He handed me books by Harry Emerson Fosdick, George Buttrick, and Leslie Weatherhead which I read avidly. He conversed with me personally about the meanings, message, and person of Jesus Christ. All of this was like gentle rain on my parched mind. All sorts of good growth resulted.

One day in my dormitory room, I read many of the references to God as a Father in Jesus' teaching. It dawned upon me that in

the Word become flesh in Jesus I had full membership in the
family of God who is my Father in the realm of heaven, which is
a revealed dimension of life here and now and forever. I ceased
to be loaded down by the burden of being fatherless, by the
desolate feelings caused by that condition. Here was the point
at which the pastor who baptized me had left me "hanging out to
dry." This was the time of my real conversion. William Lynch
and others introduced me to William James's book, *The
Varieties of Religious Experience*. Conversion became to me
just what he said it is:

> To be converted, to be regenerated, to receive grace, to
> experience religion, to gain an assurance, are so many
> phrases which denote the process, gradual or sudden, by
> which a self hitherto divided, and consciously wrong
> inferior and unhappy, becomes unified and consciously
> right superior and happy, in consequence of its firmer
> hold upon religious realities. This at least is what
> conversion signifies in general terms, whether or not we
> believe that a direct divine operation is needed to bring
> such a moral change about. (William James, *The Varieties
> of Religious Experience*, Lecture IX; New American
> Library edition, p. 157)

The Word of God, the Logos, the person of Jesus Christ, was
my redemption from feelings of inferiority. From then on I felt
it a divine imperative never to think of any human being as
inferior to me, nor, at the same time, to think of any human
being as superior to me. From then on I began to look *across* at
all people. I work at this as my daily discipline; to walk *humbly*
with God and *comradely* with people. For all of us are made in
the image of God. All of us are bought with the same price of the
death of Jesus Christ. All of us who once were "no people" are
now the "people of God."

My calling since that time at Mars Hill College has been
gently to take off the cheap price tags people place on
themselves and ask their permission to bestow the price tag
God our heavenly Parent has placed on us with a love that is

more than human love. For this nobody need walk in shame for any reason.

Since the realization of my genuine worth in Jesus Christ, I have sought to follow his command, "Call no man your father on earth, for you have one Father, who is in heaven" (Matt. 23:9). This has applied to teachers; they are my mentors and coaches, but I am not their child. It applies to people of all social classes; they are more or less affluent but not better or worse than I am. This applies to people of different races; they have different colors from mine, but they are my brothers; I am not to paternalize them. This applies to students of mine; I may have had more experience and discipline in the subject matter, but they are my comrades in learning; they are not children of mine. They have been paternalized, bureaucratized, and imperialized enough to last them by the time they get to me.

The critical theological issue in the pyramids of inferiority we build is one of idolatry. We become the slave of that or those to which or whom we feel inferior. We are called in the power of Jesus Christ to cast down, refute, and destroy the arguments of every proud obstacle to the knowledge of God (II Cor. 10:3-6). Admittedly this is iconoclastic and makes for other struggles. Nevertheless, these things are the stuff of spiritual combat.

The Blessing of the Paradox of Self-Confidence and Teachableness: An Invitation to Dialogue

As you have read this chapter, you may have sensed a strange element of intense self-confidence as an antidote for my sense of inferiority. Often it amounts to a "screwed-up courage." You have a right to say at certain points: "Methinks he doth protest too much." You yourself may be asking: "When does self-confidence become arrogance?" You push me into deeper waters of our relationship to God when you ask this question. This calls for a paradox, a seemingly contradictory opinion that is nevertheless true. If indeed God in Jesus Christ sets you and me free from a crippling sense of inferiority, then when does our self-confidence turn into arrogance? Wherein is our self-confidence balanced?

Your self-confidence and mine becomes arrogance when we forget its source. The psalmist asked the question: "From whence does my help come?" He answered: "My help comes from the LORD, who made heaven and earth." But this is too likely to become arrogance in itself; that is, we have a corner on the help that comes from the Lord and we hoard it for ourselves, doling it out in absolute demands upon other people and total inability to let God bring help to us through them. *When you and I break out of that arrogance, we become open and teachable both in our prayers before God and in our conversations with each other. You may have a dearth of mentors in your life to give you self-confidence, wisdom, and encouragement. Is it that you have a corner on the market of self-confidence, wisdom, and courage? I hope not. The paradoxical outcome of genuine self-confidence that comes from the Lord is humility—by which Jesus meant teachability, tenderness of heart, and willingness to learn from trustworthy persons.

Beneath the source of our help in God and at the point of our temptation to arrogance is your and my capacity to *trust* trustworthy people. We learn to discern between the persons who can be trusted and learned from safely and those who cannot. This is a *wise* humility. The psalmist also said: "I said in my consternation 'Men are all a vain hope'" (Ps. 116:11). The King James Version translates, "All men are liars." Some people are a vain hope and liars. But the person with self-confidence and humility knows that not all people are so.

Your and my self-confidence avoids the vinegar fate of arrogance when it instead is moved toward teachableness, tenderness of heart, and eagerness to learn from others. This produces new wine of the Spirit. You see the most vivid example of it in Jesus' encounter with the two men on the road to Emmaus. They said of the experience: "Did not our hearts burn within us while he talked to us on the road, while he opened to us the scriptures?" (Luke 24:32). Such responsiveness is a sure source of self-confidence for you and me and an equally sure antidote to arrogance, not only as we meet Jesus as Lord in our private world but also as we meet him as he reveals himself to us through some surprisingly unlikely fellow strugglers with the sense of inferiority.

3
To Be Free
from Pack Thinking

AT MARS HILL COLLEGE, one of the best friends I had was
Eugene Brissey, a fellow South Carolinian. We debated
together, we had many personal discussions of the issues of
political science. We later went from Mars Hill College to
Wake Forest College and graduated in the same class. In 1942,
he went into the Navy, was wounded, and recovered enough to
become a public relations officer for Eastern Airlines.
However, his wounds finally took his life.

Brissey stands out vividly in my memory, and especially one
of the events we shared together. We belonged to the same
leadership fraternity, one that you qualified for by achievement
and not by reason of money, political pull, or being "voted in."
On one occasion the organization was considering a group
protest by boycotting the classes of one particular professor
because of his views on war. Brissey objected. He insisted that
each of us in our own way confront the professor one by one. As
he spoke, he said: "I don't think in packs."

His metaphor comes, as you would surmise, from the way
some animals run in packs, such as wolves. I agreed with and
adopted as my own the commitment never to be enslaved to the
party lines of "pack" thinkers. This has involved me in the
lifelong struggle to be free from pack thinking. Other terms for
it are bandwagon thinking, crowd psychology, and propaganda.

It would be easy and struggle free if the resolution to resist
pack thinking were not pulled at by our necessity for com-

47

munity, the meeting of minds with others, and fellowship with our own kind. This struggle is inherent in our ambivalent needs for individuality and communion. You are caught between your need for the approval of persons who are contending with each other and your need for independent judgment, balanced wisdom, and personal integrity.

The struggle to be free of pack thinking began when I was elected president of the Baptist Student Union at Mars Hill College. For all practical purposes, the persons in Student Union offices were the only student government the school had. As long as we were functioning on our own campus, things went smoothly. However, when we went to the Southwide student retreat at Ridgecrest that summer, we met full pressure to conform to a highly organized and carefully packaged agenda for our campus activity. I listened closely and learned what these denominational officers had to say. I had no conflict with them. I simply charted our own course the way that fit our situation.

However, a civil war was going on within me. I perceived the Christian faith to be concerned with the unique personal burdens each student brought to the college within himself or herself, the kinds of personal, family, and social problems that beset one. I did not see the projection of an organization for its own sake as a top priority. Yet, this was the way the pack was going.

In the midst of this inner conflict, I began to reexamine the exact shape my destiny would take. Up to this time—the summer of 1937—I saw myself as becoming a lawyer-politician. Now all that was swept away. I had found a fresh angle of vision of my destiny in the Old and New Testaments and my experience of the Fatherhood of God and the deliverance from bondage effected by my faith in Jesus Christ. In my attempts to be a religious leader, I had found a sense of direction for my destiny under God. In the quietness of a solitary walk in the rhododendron-covered hills of North Carolina I came to a steadfast certainty both that I wanted to be a minister and that

God was inviting me to be a minister. No visions, ecstasies, or loud voices accompanied the certainty. The intelligence of the eternal God worked through his creation of my own mind to bring closure to a decision to be a minister. It was not a job, a function, a role, or a part in a drama. It was something I simply started being and becoming with the full encouragement of God. The specific focus of ministry for me was the orphaned persons, the conflict-ridden ones, those with families broken as mine was, and those who were wandering without a sense of destiny. I could not see myself as only concerned with recruiting converts to a particular denomination. At once this put me into a lonely spot in relation to those around me who were so-called evangelists out to "save" the world by their efforts, zeal, and organization.

For three or four years after that I tried hard to conform to this pattern of simplistic revivalism. The more I sought to see changes take place in people's lives through these approaches, the more unreal to me they became. I found myself at variance with older leaders for whom I had much personal respect, but with whose ideas and methods I deeply disagreed. Yet I was hard pressed to have anything better to offer than their stylized proselytism of masses of people. Sufficient good came in the lives of enough people to make me know that I could not just throw out the baby with the bath. Yet I could not forget the lack of genuine content and the neglect of my inner complexities at the time of my own profession of faith and baptism. I could not forget the lack of instruction preceding and the lack of follow-up after my baptism. Surely there was a better way. As it stood, I had only two things to go on: my lack of any better approach, and my certainty that this was not the way to go. It was the patent-medicine, over-the-counter remedy for everything that made me grope for freedom from this kind of pack thinking and acting. Surely there was a more prescriptive, individualized, and growth-oriented approach to the proclamation of the good news of Jesus Christ. This struggle to be free from pack thinking and a jingoistic, sales-pitch evangelism, therefore, was inherent in my experience of baptism and in my commitment to be a minister of the gospel. This struggle was destined to stay with me until this day. To me, accepting the struggle as a part of the terrain and the opposition was the only way to go.

Throughout my career this struggle has taken on an acute character at specific times and under specific circumstances. The struggle to be free of pack thinking epitomizes my experience as a college senior. In the fall of 1938, a contingent of students who graduated from Mars Hill went to Wake Forest College, then an all-male institution. We immediately met another remarkably dedicated and competent faculty. Their common commitment was to teach us to think independently and to provide us with the classical tools for doing so. Subject matter was a medium through which we were disciplined to think our own thoughts and to think God's thoughts after him. As Kepler said as he studied astronomy: "O God, I am thinking thy thoughts after thee."

Classical and Koine Greek, which I had begun studying at Mars Hill, became an intriguing passion. The clear, precise meanings of words, the dramatic syntax implementing in detail the functions of the individual psyche and interpersonal relations, became a discipline which I use almost daily to this day. Latin and its kinship with Roman rule and law aided me in grasping the meaning of much of the English language. Old English and Anglo-Saxon put me into sympathy with basic English as it is known through oral tradition and not through the obfuscations of much classroom gibberish. The men who taught these languages loved their work, knew us as students at a very personal level, and could call out the best in us in a gutsy and humorous way. Yet they demanded top performance and had an inspiring way of making us feel that they personally would be alarmed, wounded, and shaken if we let them down. It mattered to them that we should achieve to the outer limits of our abilities.

English literature brought Shakespeare and Milton alive for me. While reading Tennyson's *In Memoriam* I first detected the process of grief as the poet moved from the stage of shock, to disbelief, to fantasy, to despair, to stabbing memories, to a life of faith in the face of not knowing. Tennyson grieved for Arthur Hallam, his close friend. Pneumonia had that spring killed my roommate, Clyde Randolph, and I grieved for him. Concurrently with English literature I took my first course in marriage and family under the tutelage of Prof. Olin T. Binkley. He had just come to the faculty from the pastorate of the Chapel Hill Baptist Church. He had worked alongside the sociologist Ernest Groves in developing a college and university course on preparation for participating in marriage. This was one of the many national roots of present-day marriage and family therapy. Olin Binkley was my first counselor in *any* professional sense of the word. He counseled with me about my heritage, my charting of my academic work, my hopes for marriage and a family of my own, and about the need for pastors professionally educated to counsel with people about specific troubles they were enduring.

One of the most profound impressions Olin Binkley made upon me was his careful reviews of books he had read, the way he remembered the full bibliography, the statements of purpose, the methods of research, the central discoveries of the authors, etc. He was a walking computer with an amazingly wide range of knowledge.

Similarly impressive to me were the thoroughness of his preparation for his classes, the deliberateness of his style of lecturing, and the atmosphere of intellectual inquiry and personal reverence that pervaded his classroom. From my identification with him as a teacher I resolved to express my ministry through the classroom and the clinic as well as through the pulpit. Olin Binkley was my mentor and teacher, my confidant and friend. He advised me to be a teacher in psychology and philosophy. He was our premarital counselor when Pauline and I married and the best man in our wedding. Later at the Southern Baptist Theological Seminary he was my teacher in Christian Ethics and was a member of my doctoral committee. We taught together at the seminary and college levels. He coached me on the development of curriculum in the hitherto-undeveloped field of pyschology of religion and gave me support within faculties. He has been an inspiration, an older brother in Christ, an ideal teacher after whom I modeled my work, and a steadfast friend.

When it comes to independent thinking, Olin Binkley is an artist. He coolly computes evidence, uses a minimum of verbiage, and draws conclusions on the basis of evidence that marks the path of wisdom. Pack thinking is alien to him, and his wisdom has both depth and durability.

Another powerful force in my intellectual formation was A. C. Reid, professor of psychology and philosophy at Wake Forest College. His Ph.D. from Cornell was in experimental psychology under E. B. Tichenor. However, his first love was philosophical psychology. He was steeped in the history of philosophy, especially ancient Greek philosophy. Reid taught us that "philosophy is the sincere and persistent search for truth wherever manifestations of truth may be found."

Professor Reid was a rigid disciplinarian in his classroom and a taskmaster in his advanced philosophy seminars. He demanded that we read *all* of Plato's dialogues, the psychological philosophies of Aristotle, Spinoza, Hume, Descartes, Locke, William James, John Dewey, and John B. Watson. He pointed us toward Carl Jung and ignored Freud. He is a devout Christian and has taught Sunday school for decades in the Wake Forest Baptist Church. His Christian heroes to whom he introduced us were Albert Schweitzer, Rufus Jones the Quaker mystic, and William Ernest Hocking. We were expected to evaluate our own Christian beliefs by writing serious papers on several systems of philosophy: materialism, idealism, mysticism, and pragmatism. We were expected to be able to give "a reason for the hope that was in us."

Probably the most exacting study which A. C. Reid required of me was an intensive study of epistemology, i.e., theories of knowing. How does one know anything and, more than that,

how does one *know* that one knows it? In other words, what are
the sources of conviction, belief, certainty in life? This
discipline made me reexamine all that I believed. I kept that
which by specific experience I had demonstrated to be true.
Never again could I take without my own scrutiny and ex-
perimentation what someone else said was so. F. H. Giddings,
one of the pioneers in American sociology, put it into a
sentence: "I want to know if a thing is true, or is it that everyone
is simply *saying* that it is true." From this point forward I had
crossed another bridge, and burnt it, and there was no turning
back. I could never be a yea-sayer, a pack thinker, a pawn of
propaganda, a worshiper of what Bacon called the idols of the
marketplace. Prayer became to me that internal action in which
I sought to discern the intentions of God amid the hidden and
manifest persuaders with smooth rhetoric.

Another powerful person became intensely significant to me
at Wake Forest. Henlee Barnette was a classmate of mine. He
and I had both gone to college after working at Cannon Towel
Company in Kannapolis in 1936. I went to Mars Hill and he
went straight to Wake Forest from the start. We reunited when
I went to Wake Forest in 1938 as a junior. We took Greek,
Latin, Shakespeare, psychology, and philosophy together I
took Milton and Tennyson; he took American literature. He
had a similar cotton-mill heritage to my own, although he had
worked ten years in the mills, whereas I had worked only two.
He had started to work when he was thirteen. Becoming a page
in the Senate had given me a temporary reprieve. He had
worked at night and gone to high school during the day.

Immediately we were fellow pilgrims, and our comradeship
has lasted to this very day. We work together as fellow
professors at the School of Medicine of the University of
Louisville. Prior to this we taught together at the Southern
Baptist Theological Seminary, he in Christian ethics and I in
psychology of religion and pastoral care, for over twenty-five
years.

Henlee Barnette became my colleague in resisting the pack

thinking that Southern Baptists, Southern culture, and pseudo intellectuals pushed our way. Neither he nor I was any more interested in the clubbiness of liberals than we were in the storm-troop tactics of fundamentalists. Yet we were eager for even-ground dialogue with both packs. Our sense of humor has been the sustaining lubricant of our friendship with each other.

This comradeship has been an intellectual quest in which we mutually informed each other about the technical inner detail of our specialties. At the same time we have been spiritual confidants and confessors to each other, providing authentic spiritual direction to each other in times of grief, pain, illness, political adversity, and in times of celebration, achievement, and triumph. Anybody can commiserate with you. As you know, persons of great character can celebrate your successes without envy, jealousy, and greed. Henlee Barnette has that greatness of character and heart.

The weapons for dealing with pack thinking were forged, tempered, and sharpened at Wake Forest College. The full-scale battle was ahead of me. I became a veteran at this struggle to be free of pack thinking in several crucial situations.

Graduation from Wake Forest College came May 27, 1940. We sat in bleacher seats at the stadium while heavy storm clouds with flashes of lightning gathered over us. The rumble of distant thunder was symbolic. Hitler had invaded Poland on September 1, 1939. Forty infantry divisions and fourteen panzer divisions blitzkrieged that brave but beleaguered country. By the time of our graduation France was on the verge of the defeat; the defeat was formalized on June 12, 1940. May 27 itself was a fateful day for the British against Hitler's Luftwaffe as Dunkirk harbor was put out of use. The British evacuation had already begun on May 26. By June 4, 1940, 198,000 British and 140,000 French and Belgian troops had been saved. Most of their battle equipment had to be abandoned. Of 41 destroyers, 6 were sunk and 19 were damaged.

This was the context of our graduation with the gathering

storm of war around us. My work with A. C. Reid had been
effective enough that I was asked to stay on as an instructor in
psychology and philosophy. I would be allowed to take a
pastorate if I could find the work. The pay was not enough to
support even a single man. I turned to a retired professor of
religion, Dr. W. R. Cullom, who was pastor of the Spring Hope
Baptist Church at Spring Hope, North Carolina, about
thirty-five miles from the campus.

Providentially, the rural churches at the Peachtree and Bunn
communities, surrounding Spring Hope from the west and the
north, were both without a pastor. Through the influence and
ministry of introduction of Dr. Cullom, I was asked by these
churches to be their pastor. I eagerly accepted. I began work
with them in June 1940, teaching at Wake Forest during the
week and serving the churches full-time in the summer and
part-time in the winter.

I had never had courses in preaching, church management,
and pastoral care. However, I had the continuous coaching of
O. T. Binkley and W. R. Cullom. They gave me clinical
supervision of my work for the two years I was pastor there.
A. C. Reid gave me supervision of my teaching and his point of
view as a lay Christian concerning my care of my people.

Yet the party-line thought of Southern Baptists was that the
be-all and end-all of a Southern Baptist pastor was to function as
an evangelist who increased the size of the church. Within this
party line I set out to find *all* the people in the community. I
visited everyone in the geographic reach of the churches.
When I had finished visiting them, I started over again. My
main reason for visiting them was to get them to come to
church. If they had never professed faith in Jesus Christ, my
simple appeal was that they accept him as their Savior and be
baptized, and I promised to continue to follow their spiritual
growth. *If they did not do this, then I continued to be interested
in them as their friend and pastor*. This is where I broke with
the pack thinking of Southern Baptists. I did not restrict my
ministry to people who came to church. I visited tenant

farmers, alcoholics, those with sickness or grief. The dispossessed situation of blacks hit me hard as I visited. I went to the barns where people worked with tobacco, to the stores where they gathered, to the small towns on Saturday afternoons, and to cotton and tobacco markets where they sold their crops.

I continued my visitation for a third time around. Then is when I broke out of the old wineskins of pack thinking about being a pastor. I began to see and think with these people in *their* terms and not my own as a sort of salesperson for the church. I found a family who had a mongoloid child whom they kept strapped in a rocker. I found an alcoholic father who had a daughter who was pregnant out of wedlock. He never came to church but he invited me to his home for dinner. Before he asked me to ask the blessing he said: "Mr. Oates, we raised everything on this table ourselves, except the sugar, salt, coffee, and pepper, of course." Then I thanked God for the food and the loving hands that had raised it, cooked it, and served it. I was amazed that the daughter gave birth to her baby in the home and the child was accepted as a part of the family as a matter of love. Church members thought this was sort of "trashy," but the grandfather and grandmother of the baby did not; nor did they think the daughter was an outcast. These things puzzled me, but I continued to visit the new baby the same way I did all the others.

I saw many cancer patients for the first time in my life. They all died at home, not in hospitals. The funerals were from the homes. We had neither intensive care units nor funeral homes as we now do. People sat up all night with the corpse so the family could sleep a little. Food was brought and people visited with each other in droves. These cancer patients worked with tobacco plants, smoked or chewed tobacco. I wondered then if there was a connection.

Another family was composed of all men. There had been no daughters, only three sons. The mother had died prior to my being pastor. The father had been an active church member and a deacon prior to her death. Upon her death he dropped out of church along with all three of the sons. They did all their own cooking and cleaning—such as it was. A retarded brother of the father, uncle of the sons, lived with them. The common report of several neighbors who were very active in the church was that these men had "taken to bootlegging whiskey." The church people felt that they should be confronted about this. I asked that this matter be left to me.

I had had uncles and a brother-in-law in South Carolina who were moonshiners. I had been present when "revenuers" or officials assigned to policing the illegal manufacturing and black-marketing of alcohol caught, jailed, and fined them.

Instead of accusing these men of bootlegging, I began visiting them twice a week at different times of the day and days of the week. I told them I wanted to get to know them better and especially to know how they had lost their wife and mother. I wanted to know how they were managing to get along without her care. They made a place for me in their hearts, as Paul had asked of the Corinthians (see II Cor. 7:2-4, NEB). I learned about the fear of the father and sons that the retarded brother and uncle would marry a prostitute in the nearby town with whom he consorted. They thought he was too "addled in the head" to be married. He and I talked together and I discouraged the plan. He followed my advice.

But the most important effect was that these men gave up their bootlegging without my ever mentioning it to them. They began occasionally returning to church. However, the gnawing loneliness over the loss of their wife and mother was still with them when I left the area.

The most dramatic event occurred when a little six-year-old boy at vacation Bible school came to me and said "Dr. Cheeves wants you to come to see my ma. She's sick." I went with the child to his home. The mother was in bed. She said that the doctor told her she needed someone to talk with about her troubles. He recommended me. I listened to her story of her troubles. I told her I needed to pray about her troubles and to talk with her doctor. I had prayed with her and told her not to despair; God was with us.

I conferred with the doctor and he said she was genuinely sick with stomach, intestinal, and blood pressure problems. These were aggravated by her fear of her husband, who was a heavy drinker. He encouraged me to continue to see her, to get acquainted with each of her children, and to try to understand what caused the husband to need so much booze. He urged me to listen, observe, and pray with them.

These things I did, and I was amazed to see that her health improved, her husband's sadness lifted and his drinking decreased, and her children began to laugh and play again. I stayed in touch with this family even after I left the pastoral charge there. The mother fully recovered. We all gave God thanks for his work in our lives.

Not long after this, Dr. Cheeves was called into the military. He, upon leaving, urged me to give myself to studying and teaching about the relation of the ministry and medicine. He said: "It's the wave of the future."

Pack thinking about the Christian witness focuses on the church as an institution that people serve. Salvation becomes a package of right words and phrases to say. The pastor is taught, prompted, urged, and paid to "traverse sea and land" to make proselytes (Matt. 23:15). I have no inhibition in forthrightly proclaiming the good news of God in Jesus Christ for the redemption of persons. However, I turn again and again to Jesus' own manner of resisting the package thinking of his day and pinpointing the good news of the Kingdom at the site of peoples' most personal fears, burdens, complex relationships, illnesses, and loneliness.

In kaleidoscopic fashion other dramatic crises of my life have centered down upon the agony and ecstasy of the struggle to be free of pack thinking. In 1943, I entered a theological school that had a closed curriculum which *everybody* was required to fit into. The combat veterans returning from World War II brought the same demand for person-centered approaches to the pastoral ministry. Christian ethics, pastoral care, and a wide variety of electives in theology were the result.

In 1948, a whole group of young professors, of whom I was one, were added to the faculty. It was easy for the "young Turks" to become a pack. Increasingly, I found myself detaching myself from the pack, much to the consternation of the young and the puzzlement of the older. This eventuated in a polarized conflict in 1958 that resulted in the resignation of twelve younger professors. I could not be a part of the pack. Neither could I be a tool of the power structure that remained.

In the 1950s and 1960s, also, we were caught in the nationwide civil rights movement. Whereas I took individual stands in specific cases for blacks', women's, and handicapped persons' rights, I have never felt at ease in lifting from these persons their own responsibilities for exerting their efforts to achieve personal freedom from exploitation.

Probably the most vivid encounters I have had with pack thinking have outstripped those in the confines of the Southern Baptist Convention. They have been in the field of clinical pastoral education and the hand-in-glove relationship our movement has with psychiatry and psychotherapy. When I entered this field in 1944, the Freudian psychoanalytic frame of reference was the going thing. I learned this approach well, had extensive psychoanalytic therapy in the course of my two years of supervised clinical pastoral education. I had a remarkably wise and thought-provoking supervisor in Rev. Ralph Bonacker, who himself had been through analysis and who had a firm grasp of Reformed and Augustinian theology. Yet when I got to Chicago and Elgin State Hospital, I found men in charge of the program who were slavishly following English and Pearson's book *Emotional Problems of Living* in a superficial way. They were in severe conflict with Anton Boisen because he resisted the bandwagon enthusiasm for popularized versions of Freud. My approach was to dig out all of the original writings of Freud himself and to do a historical and source criticism of his teachings. My doctoral committee approved this as the subject for my dissertation: "The Significance of the Work of Sigmund Freud for the Christian Faith." Many made light of it. However, my graduate committee took both the thesis and me personally very seriously and tempered my work with remarkable wisdom and perspective.

Throughout my career, the field of pastoral care has moved from one psychotherapy bandwagon to another. After Freud came Carl Rogers. Concurrent with Carl Rogers came Wilhelm Reich. Then came Harry Stack Sullivan. Then came Erik Erikson. Then came Ekstein and Wallerstein's theories on the teaching and learning of psychotherapy. Then a whole pyrotechnics of "pop" psychologies burst on the horizon: transactional analysis, integrity therapy, Gestalt therapy, encounter groups, noöthetic counseling, etc. The present concern is with systems theory.

My approach has been to read closely the primary sources of the gurus of psychotherapy and to submit them to a historical analysis of their sources and the tributaries of the influences that brought them into being. Likewise, I have studied closely the particular population of people with whom the particular guru was working while formulating his or her theory. At no point have I accepted wholesale the teachings and methods of any of them. Nor have I been an eclectic, picking and choosing this and that from each of them.

To the contrary, I have used the criteria of Reformation and free-church theology for assessing the "trendiness" of each wave of crowd thinking. I came very near to stating fully my own personal stance about all these things in my book entitled *Protestant Pastoral Counseling* (1962). The book is still a serious challenge to stereotyping of the ministry by psychoanalytic assumptions. It put the work of pastoral counseling in relation to the life of the Spirit, the life of the church, and the hope of the Kingdom of God. It still provides my own theoretical base for pastoral counseling and psychotherapy.

Since I have been a professor in a medical school in a public university, I have seen innumerable polarizations of contending groups on crucial issues. It has been my native inclination to seek to maintain working relationships with all sides of social contentions. The truth *has* to be somewhere *among* these forces and no one of them has a corner on it. Life is too ambiguous and ambivalent for that. Christian love to me is the power of the Spirit of Christ working *among* people to overcome this ambiguity and ambivalence by bringing to pass a humility and reconciliation in the place of arrogance and power plays.

One might assume, since I have for eight years been a professor of psychiatry in a school of medicine, that modern clinical psychiatry has become a bandwagon for me. *Au contraire!* The chairman of the department, John Schwab, M.D., at the outset of my tenure as a full professor, said: "You are our one pastor and theologian. Do not put your own lamp under a bushel." I find that I am expected to be expert in *all* of the theological disciplines. I am accepted and respected for a steady distinctiveness. Intense debates over different treatment modalities are waged all around me by differing psychiatrists. I read intensively the published research on these controversies about the efficacy of neuroleptic medications, the amounts of medication, shock therapy, lithium therapy, short-term crisis hospitalization versus longer-term milieu therapy, and so on ad infinitum. I used a historical analytic approach to my own conclusions concerning these live issues. Here again, I find the methods of historical criticism that I first learned in the study of the Bible to be useful in maintaining independence of thought in this environment, too.

Someone reading what I have said here about the struggle to be free of pack thinking may assume that I am making a case for being a "loner," an isolated individual who is afraid to take a stand. That is one reaction of some people who resist pack thinking, i.e., to pronounce a curse on all sides of controversial issues, "to shut oneself within oneself and to let the devil pipe his own." Yet that is no temptation for me. I regularly find myself in the thick of the battle among contending factions. The very discipline of pastoral counseling and psychotherapy calls for this. To the contrary, I insist on a multilateral partiality instead of a unilateral partiality. This focuses my identity as a minister of reconciliation in the name of Jesus Christ.

For example, I found myself in this position during the Vietnam War. I could readily see that we as a nation had shilly-shallied ourselves into an undeclared war that should never have been. I could identify with patriotic young men who volunteered to fight our country's war. My own son Bill was one who did so. Yet, with him, I could not repress my admiration for the Vietcong who saw themselves as fighting a civil war to unify their country in spite of a powerful outside force in the United States military effort. I could even see that Ho Chi Minh was unwittingly the instrument of God teaching us as a nation the limits of human power. I sat with all my people and wept as we blew taps on a lost cause when Saigon fell and became Ho Chi Minh City.

The person who commits himself or herself to the struggle to be free of pack thinking, propaganda, and party-line clichés does best to take a stand for justice for all and mercy for all. Yet this places him or her in the role of a reconciler, a peacemaker, a negotiator, an interlocutor. The hazard is that of being despised by all contending forces for not taking sides. There is a quantum leap of difference between taking sides and taking a stand as a minister of reconciliation. Jesus said: "Blessed are the peacemakers, for they shall be called sons of God" (Matt. 5:9). After forty-two years of this, I can say with gratitude that to know one is a child of God is a source of peace in itself. However, my sense of sardonic or even gallows humor says: "Yes, Lord! But that is not *all* one will be called by any means!"

The "Crowd" vs. the "Community": An Invitation to Dialogue

The crowd of the popular mind is always seeking an escape from the disciplined struggle to be a person in one's own right.

It is easier for you and me to fade into the woodwork or wallpaper of the prevalent opinion. But Martin Buber was right when he said that the idea of community must be guarded against all contamination by sentimentality or emotionalism. The community of struggle against pack thinking is, as Buber says, "community of tribulation, and only because of that, community of spirit; community of toil and, only because of that, community of salvation" (*The Way of Response*, p. 155; ed. by Nahum N. Glatzer; Schocken Books, 1966).

Yet you and I have nothing to offer a community if we have no individuality of our own. A crowd is the bundling together of beings with no sense of apartness, selfhood, and uniqueness. A community is a fellowship of people of working faith who have both a clear-cut sense of individuality and a need to have fellowship with and learn from other persons who are distinct selves in their own right. Our main claim to partnership is that we bring our own generativity to it. Otherwise we are "hangers on," with no growth apart from the nutriment that the crowd gives. To be such is a parasitic existence not worthy of you or me. Hence we can derive the maxim: Be yourself; commit yourself to the organism of the body of Christ composed of members with differing gifts, to perform the works of love to God and neighbor.

T. S. Eliot saw deeply into the struggle for individual autonomy. He saw its ambiguous nature. He said that even the lonely hermit monk praying alone in the desert prayed in the context of the body of Christ, the church. My struggle to be free of pack thinking at base is that kind of prayer. You and I do not see this struggle as an effort to be asocial. To the contrary, we commit ourselves to the fellowship of humankind through the power of the Spirit to enable us to break the bread of the body of Christ and drink the wine of the blood of Christ in gladness and singleness of heart. This is a communion and not a herding of people together under the partisan cries of this, that, or the other party line. Paul describes this struggle in his First Letter to the Corinthians. He complains that some people say, "I belong to Paul" or "I belong to Cephas." For this reason Paul baptized very few, as he told them, "lest any one should say that you were baptized in my name" (I Cor. 1:12-17). This is the genesis of party cries, crowd thinking, pack thinking. Freedom from it is not to be found in baptizing or in various packaged sales items, all of which deny the cross of Christ of its power. It is enough to be and become according to the gospel, and to convey the good news of Jesus Christ.

4
To Be Free
of Loneliness

THE HERITAGE of poverty, the uneasy sense of inferiority,
and the stubborn streak that insisted on independence of
thought have added up to loneliness for me. All of my life I have
experienced loneliness as inherent in my total being. The very
experience of writing, which has been equally a part of my
being, is one way of having a sense of community with you as my
reader. Yet, at the same time, writing, like practicing as a
musician, is a lonely function. No book ever got written in a
crowd. Sometimes books are written by committees. I have
been a part of such groups. But the end product is a consensus,
a least common denominator of the thought of the group, not
the thought of some person striking out on his or her own at
considerable risk of eccentricity.

One of the loneliest yet most profound books I have read is
Dag Hammarskjöld's *Markings*. In it he wryly remarks: "If
even dying is to be made a social function, then, please, grant
me the favor of sneaking out on tiptoe without disturbing the
party" (p. 73; tr. by Leif Sjöberg and W. H. Auden; Alfred A.
Knopf, 1968). The genuinely lonely person, it seems, both feels
the struggle to be free of the pain of loneliness and at the same
time embraces it lovingly as his or her destiny. Such is my
feeling of it anyhow.

Consequently I can speak of both the struggle to be free of the
pain inherent in loneliness and the sense of destiny that
prompts my preference for loneliness.

The Pain of Loneliness

Being little among grown-ups can be a painfully lonely feeling. For a two-year-old and a five-year-old, watching their mother and father in a physical fight is loneliness at the edge of the abyss of terror. Being little and teased unmercifully by older siblings set me apart from them very early. Being little and left to my own devices for whole twelve-hour days made loneliness a part of my being between the ages of two and six. Forays into neighbors' homes, being fed coffee with sugar, and canned milk with bread in it (a concoction my grandmother called "composey"), and running to meet my mother at 6:15 in the evening—these events punctuated an otherwise lonely day, day after day. Yet I do not remember this as pain so much as it was longing. I have no memory of any playmates in this period; nor do I remember particularly wanting playmates. I spent most of my thoughts trying to figure out what the adults in my world were up to and all about.

The pain came in my search for a father. I recall that someone attempted to break into our house when I was about three. The intruder was driven away. The windows were boarded up after that. No one discussed it much. I was convinced that it was my father coming to get me. I never told anyone what I thought. After all, it was in that same time span that he had come to see us one Sunday. He took me for a ride on Paris Mountain near Greenville. He nearly ran off the road at one point. He had one arm around me and the other on the steering wheel. He just *might* have wanted me. Many years later I learned from my sister that he promised her to send her to school if she would come with him. She wept and refused because she felt all her life she had to take care of mother.

The search for a father came dramatically to an end when I concluded, as I have earlier said, that Jesus commanded us to call no man father, for our heavenly Father is our Father. Yet somehow I searched for human beings who cared for me for my own sake. I deliberately scanned the world of men to find

persons worth trusting, copying, listening to, and whom I
might even risk becoming like. These have included the streetcar motorman; Mr. Dowling, a seventh-grade science teacher;
Mr. Biffle, my Senate page boss; Prof. R. L. Moore, president
of Mars Hill College; William Lynch, pastor of the Mars Hill
Baptist Church; O. T. Binkley, A. C Reid, and W. R. Cullom at
Wake Forest College; Harold Tribble, J. B. Weatherspoon,
and Gaines S. Dobbins of the Southern Baptist Theological
Seminary; Lewis J. Sherrill of the Louisville Presbyterian
Theological Seminary and later of Union Theological Seminary
in New York; S. Spafford Ackerly, then professor and chairman
of psychiatry at the University of Louisville School of Medicine;
Edwin S. Gheens, a businessman and mentor of mine in
Louisville. These men were and still are very vital beings or
spirits in my life. In my meditations even today, I reflect on
wisdom that comes through these incarnate media of the grace
of God to fill the void created by loss of my father. Painful
loneliness drove me to seek out teachers who would assuage
that pain by their example, their acceptance of me as a person
with intelligence and courage enough to use it as a hammer and
forge to work out my destiny under God. It was that painful void
which drove me from within to seek them out. It was the sheer
providence of God coupled with their own commitment to
younger persons that caused them to be there at just the right
time and place in my pilgrimage.

These persons came into my life. Yes. Then again, I actively
brought them into my life out of a deep sense of void,
emptiness, and loneliness that seems to have been there from
the outset. I never suffered a *broken* attachment from my
father. There simply was *no* attachment at all except in the
imagination of what I would want an attachment to be and the
kind of person to whom I would choose to attach my devotion.

The people I have mentioned were all disciplined persons;
they were leaders; they were professionals at what they did;
they lived according to the intrinsic ethic of their professions;
they were productive personalities. Hebrews 13:7 advises:

"Remember your leaders, consider the outcome of their life." This I have done. Yet these leaders were such as to hold me steady in life with an awareness of their trust in me. In the main, all of them were teachers. They were outstanding lecturers and classroom geniuses in many instances. This was not what made them different for me. The difference was that they had time for conversation with me on a one-to-one basis. It could well be that my aggressive demands for this caused them to take time. I do not think so, although I am sure I pestered them. Rather, the ideas they formulated in the classroom were pursued more intently in the mind-wrestling discussions we had outside class.

These men never paternalized me, although they filled much of the void of my fatherlessness. Instead, they treated me as having sense and encouraged me to use it as an adult—younger than they, of course—not as a child. Since having been a father myself for thirty-four years, I have wished that my sons had had access to teachers like this. In a few instances they have had such access, but not with the regularity I did. Then, too, they have not had the void to fill that I did. Yet no father can take the place of another adult outside the family in the role of mentor to his sons or daughters, can he? Or is it the pain of loneliness that creates those "out of the family" mentorships?

For me, not only the men teachers in my life unshackled the bondage of a certain kind of loneliness; also, certain women teachers were liberators for me. I met most of them in elementary school and high school—Miss Tillman, Mrs. Geiger, Mrs. Mims. In junior college, Miss Pierce was my mentor in English. However, they were *distant* ideals of the *educated* mother to me. I loved my mother, but there was always mystery and distance there. This applied to women teachers. In the early years of my life, educated and refined women were cultural supplements to the secure love I felt from my grandmother, my sister, and my mother. As I grew to professional maturity I found a conversational dialogue with women who dedicated their lives to the cultural enhancement of the city of Louisville. Four in particular have been comrades in that kind of cultural enhancement. One was Mrs. Minnie Wheeler, who was involved in the spiritual care of many of the wealthy victims of the Great Depression. She sought my professional assistance in seeing to it that they were wisely served. Another was Mrs. Jean Tachau, who founded and nurtured for many years the Planned Parenthood Clinic of Louisville. Also, Mrs. Mary Jo Gheens Hill was until her death a very personal mentor of my wife, Pauline, and a creative financier of libraries which we have sought to furnish with primary sources of research value. Mrs. Amelia Brown Frazier has been a comrade in the pastoral ministry of prayer for the sick, the handicapped, the dispossessed, and the acutely lonely people of our city.

These men and women have been my liberators from the loneliness that is inherent in my being. They have been to me what Gardner Murphy aptly calls "mediators of culture." They have been instruments of Providence in shaping me, a person born without privilege. They gave me an educated cultural context, a language with which to break out of loneliness into becoming a person who deliberately chose to be like them. Thomas Wolfe wrote a letter to one of his public school teachers, Margaret Roberts. It portrays my feelings about the persons I have described here:

> Dear Mrs. Roberts:
> . . . You say that no one *outside* my family loves me more than Margaret Roberts. Let me rather say the exact truth:—that no one *inside* my family loves me as much, and only one other person, I think, in all the world loves me as much. My book is full of ugliness and terrible pain—and I think moments of a great and soaring beauty. In it (will you forgive me?) I have told the story of one of the most beautiful people I have ever known as it touched on my own life. I am calling that person Margaret Leonard. I was without a home—a vagabond since I was seven—with two roofs and no home. I moved inward on that house of death and tumult from room to little room,

as the boarders came with their dollar a day, and their constant rocking on the porch. My overloaded heart was bursting with its packed weight of loneliness and terror; I was strangling, without speech, without articulation, in my own secretions—groping like a blind sea-thing with no eyes and a thousand feelers toward light, toward life, toward beauty and order, out of that hell of chaos, greed, and cheap ugliness—and then I found you, when else I should have died, you mother of my spirit who fed me with light. Do you think that I have forgotten? Do you think I ever will? You are entombed in my flesh, you are in the pulses of my blood, the thought of you makes a great music in me—and before I come to death, I shall use the last thrust of my talent—whatever it is—to put your beauty into words. . . . (*The Letters of Thomas Wolfe*, ed. by Elizabeth Nowell, pp. 122f.; Charles Scribner's Sons, 1956)

The pain of loneliness, however, was and is for me more than the emotional supplementation of past deprivations in my home and my culture. For me it has always had distinct social class scope to it. My integrity coheres in some of the cardinal values of my original heritage of poverty. I insist on direct encounter with persons with whom I am at odds. Time and culture have only served to temper this with a skillful calibration of the form of initiative I take—at a casual bump-into contact with the other person, by letter, by telephone, by visit, etc. In a middle- and upper-class world even this is a strange way of acting. It puts you in a singularly lonely life-style.

Furthermore, as a cotton-mill lad I learned *not* to be a joiner. In my college and seminary years I found, for example, that though I graded the papers of the students in the "English Club," I was never invited to join the club. If I had been asked, I would probably have refused. As a Christian the only group that I have ever joined without much resistance has been a Baptist church. Yet I have doubts about whether indeed the fishermen, housewives, tax collectors, customs officers, etc., of

Jesus' day knew anything about "joining" a church as we know it today. Neither Jesus nor Paul baptized (John 4:2, I Cor. 1:14). New Testament Christians certainly did not decide issues on a "majority rules" basis. In this sense, I am more in harmony with the Quakers.

In the professional societies to which I belong, my dues are paid up and I am a "card-carrying member." However, my basic certification I perceive to be my ordination as a Christian pastor. My "joining" and being an approved supervisor is strictly a way of serving my students; it is not my "church" or my main reason for being by any stretch of the imagination. This may seem to be a standoffishness to others. I can see how to them it would seem so. To me the fact is that I am not much of a joiner, and I am a very poor committee person and the worst of officeholders in organizations. This is woven into the cloth by my heritage and is not a pose that I strike to impress anyone. As for conventions, I am starkly appalled by the waste of money, time, energy, etc., they perpetrate. The whole set of objectives could be achieved more simply, austerely, and with less confusion. If the meeting is purely for the exploration of an important topic of research, inquiry, and the sharing of a fellowship of ideas, then I can "get with the program." However, I notice that such gatherings are attended by tens, or by one or two hundred, and not by thousands. But even these are not my chosen ways of learning. I prefer to read the research materials and discuss them with authors on a one-to-one basis or by correspondence. I see this as a result of my inherent antipathy to being a joiner and as a result of having gotten my whole high school education outside of a classroom setting, quite alone.

Yet this education and that which followed it made a stranger of most of my being to my native people. It certainly did not make me superior to them, better than them, or any such thing. It just plain made me the oddball in the crowd when at home. Conversely, my stubborn attachment to some of their best values has made me travel in an orbit apart from the social-class climbing, joining, impressing, selling, and posturing that I find in churches, in the professions, and in business.

Consequently, when the counterculture of the 1960s and early 1970s began (with the death of John Kennedy) and abruptly ended (with the deaths of Kent State students) I found myself "at home" with their challenge of conspicuous consumerism, with their return to simplicity of life-style, and with their challenge of the wastefulness of American life. The "war on poverty" was won by poverty, and the ethics of poverty imploded into the middle and upper classes. The lasting effects of the counterculture are still with us; but the end of the Vietnam War and the passing of the years have shown how few of the counterculture enthusiasts really meant it and how many were simply "joiners" looking for a pack to run with. When the crowd thinned out, though, some truly free spirits survived the exodus. With these I find a gentle and uncrowded fellowship though they are half my age.

A pair of these persons is Thomas Chapman and his wife, Brenda. They have planted their lives in a rural community where he barters pastoral counseling for whatever he needs with those who have no money. He often works in the fields alongside farmers for money. He preaches in various rural churches of the territory. He teaches part-time in a nearby college. He has the confidence of professional people who turn to him as a counselor. They pay him money. Brenda and he have a garden and have worked out a comity agreement with the squirrels, rabbits, and deer that populate the area so that the garden will be left alone and the animals will be fed as friends. They know what loneliness is. Yet they know what deep friendship is. They come to see me at the Medical Center occasionally. On one occasion Brenda sent a picnic basket with Tom for lunch for us in my office. I go for a day and teach a class with him at a nearby college. Tom puts his feelings into words. He too speaks of loneliness:

TWO A.M.

To be alone with oneself is to find,
not loneliness, but alone,
in . . . . solitude.

It is so frightening to face
the alone moment,
to experience the multiplicity
of your one "me."

The direction of your "alone"
often crosses the path of loneliness,
but it leads to the goal of solitude.

Seek those moments in the wilderness
            alone.
Even if it takes forty days?

Then, as both he and I struggled together in agony over the
Vietnam War during my own son's tour of duty in the war, he
wrote:

TO BEAR THAT BURDEN FOR AN HOUR

To bear that burden for an hour,
a moment,
just one second for you
I wish sometimes that gift were mine.
If we all for one moment in life
could lift that pain
from the shoulders of another.

In your pain I feel the suffering
of the millions who scream
as the bombs fall,
as the torch is set,
as the flesh burns away.

Oh the tears that must flow
from your soul
as you see so much pain.

Then I saw you another day,
and you smiled at me;
and I heard you laugh
with a dear friend.
And I laughed too.

(WEO)
December 1, 1972

(The two poems quoted above are from Thomas William
Chapman, *I saw a bird the other day. It flew.* Copyright
Thomas William Chapman 1973. Author's edition limited
to 500 signed copies. Used by permission.)

The pain of loneliness went through a transitional state as I
sought to relate myself to women my own age. Having been
raised by three women—my mother, my grandmother, and my
sister—I very early had a quaint relationship to girls. Let me
explain the quaintness.

When I was in the second grade, there was a particularly
pretty little girl named Virginia. All the little second-grade boys
were captivated by her beauty, myself included. Two of the
boys in particular developed a plan. They asked me to join
them. They were going to waylay her on the way home and
make her let them "cut" her, by which they meant they would
force her to have sexual relations with them. (You say: "Now
really! *Second-graders?*" I say: "Yes! Your doubts show that you
did not grow up to be married at fifteen-sixteen and have babies
by seventeen or eighteen." Nor is the new morality quite so
new!) I came to her defense. I told them I would have none of it
and that I would both beat the lard out of them and report them
to the principal if they touched her. They left her alone. She
never knew about it. Six years later, at the age of thirteen, upon
coming home for Christmas from Washington, I called her for a
date. I took her a gift. She was the epitome of beauty to me. I
never required anything of her. I reverenced her. She was to be
admired, respected, and protected—never used for my own
sexual gratification.

This was the *gentle* thing to be and to do. I had as much sexual libido and concern for women as anyone, but the need to protect, revere, and be respected by them held it in check. Then, too, I had a quiet, burning ambition for an education. I knew it was a long way from then through college. My power drives were stronger than my sex needs. Ambition inflated by being a page outdistanced any sexual urge of mine well past my twenty-second year.

Three forces—a genuine reverence for any girl I knew, a genuine fear of the consequences of being sexually active, and an overwhelming ambition to get an education—served to make me a lonely person when others around me were attaching themselves to girl friends. I had one short-lived crush on a girl in the town of Greenville, but my ferrying back and forth to Washington broke that up quickly.

All the way through college my relationship with girls was one of care and companionship, but uncommitment. I was working many hours to make enough money to stay in school. I was intensely absorbed in studying. Time with girls was a rarity and a much-coveted luxury. In several very meaningful relationships, I shrank back from commitment because of my own sense of ethical responsibility not to create the illusion of a sentimental romance when I myself was often able to afford only one meal a day, sleeping in very run-down quarters, and spending every available hour in the libraries. Yet I cherish the conversations I had with several women students at women's colleges near Wake Forest College.

The outcome of this quasi-celibate life was another kind of loneliness. I did not feel that any woman could possibly love a person with such a strange mixture of poverty mentality, political acumen, and scholarly preoccupation. My life being such a mishmash seemed to repel girls who had time for me. I came across as a mixture of uncomfortableness, arrogance, and strangeness to them, as I remember it. For some of them I sensed a sibling-like need to be my rival in academic excellence. To me competition was not workable, because they simply had not studied the subject matter that I had. Their work in music, art, and mathematics intrigued me. The one woman whom I admired most, trusted most profoundly, and held in tenderest regard was a University of North Carolina music major. She was a coloratura soprano with superlative ability. She too was "starving" her way through university. She too had long-range goals that precluded marriage anytime soon. We could converse profoundly about our separate interests and enjoy a tender and responsible friendship without playing the mating game. For neither of us was it the mating season. She continued her work at the Juilliard School of Music in New York. I knew she had the same "lonely long-distance runner" syndrome I had, and she knew that I did. It was a shared loneliness, if there can be such a thing. She was an emerging professional person and so was I. Yet she had a remarkable ability to appreciate other people's expertise, because, I think, she had a real experience of what a merciless discipline that expertise demanded. She never played courtship and marriage games with our comradeship; nor did I ever demand that she risk herself in sex relations with me. I have never been able to separate sexual intercourse from total commitment for any outcome it might have for the woman. This professional woman became a prototype of the kind of friend I have found in many disciplined professional women. This protectiveness of women and discipline of myself has no "goody two-shoes" meaning for me. Rather, I think it simply means that I was victimized by being the child of a man who abandoned my mother. I very early became protective of my mother, grandmother, and sister. Therefore, I would never put a woman at that kind of risk for my own self-gratification to leave her to live with the results of both our behavior. It is simply a matter of a sense of justice and injustice, not sexual purity or impurity. Nevertheless, this stance provided me with a basis for being related creatively with many women after I was married without threatening my covenant with my wife.

The consequences of this conviction made considerable

loneliness for me. The crowd was going in several other directions. Likewise, economic readiness for marriage was a long way off for me. This situation did not abate until two years after I finished college.

In the summer of 1941, I was, as I have indicated, pastor of Peachtree and Bunn Baptist Churches. I had never experienced being a part of a church as a fellowship of people until I became a pastor. The church I had known was primarily a place where other people "got saved," not a community of kindred spirits who cared for each other and cherished the corporate relationships within the church. In both these rural churches, the latter was intensely true. They knew each other by name; they kept up with each other's well-being; they celebrated the ingathering of the crops; they visited with each other at the tobacco curing ovens during curing season; they took turns helping each other get the work done if someone was sick or had simply had bad luck of other kinds; they had compassion for each other and celebrated God's good gifts with each other.

The remarkable thing about these people was that they accepted me wholeheartedly. I remember the first Sunday I went to preach at Peachtree. I got there early. A man was standing on the steps. He greeted me: "Rice is my name; what's yours?" I said: "Oates is my name." He said: "Are you kidding me?" I said: "No, Mr. Rice, Oates *is* my name and I wouldn't go against the grain with you for anything in the world!" We laughed heartily together. Laughter was a joyous exercise for these people. Yet we mourned together too. During my first year there, I conducted twenty-two funerals. We saw much illness, death, and grief. Some of these funerals were of sons who were killed in World War II. We wept together. However, the most vivid impression and memory of the faces of the people in my first pastorate was their joyous laughter, their well-turned stories, and the way they insisted on joy in living. Theirs was the *joie de vivre* in the face of stresses of all kinds. I had found an extended family among them. They gave me honor as their pastor, gently suggesting ways of improving my work but never criticizing or carping at me. For the first time in my life I did not feel acutely alone and lonely.

Each Sunday when I preached, there was one face that kept impressing me after the first several months there. She stood out from the crowd with her dainty appearance, her beautiful clothing, her picture-brimmed hats, her talkative brown eyes, and an amazing dimple in her left cheek. I do not remember meeting her at church. However, I was driving to the home of Mrs. J. R. May for dinner one noonday. (They ate the main meal at noon and rested from farm work in the heat of the day.) I came upon a horse and rider in the middle of the road. The rider was a woman who had long, brown, wavy hair, and wore work clothes. I eased by in my car to keep from frightening the horse. I went on to Mrs. May's home.

As we all came into the dining room, I recognized the person before me as the girl who had been on the horse. However, she was no longer in slacks and an old shirt. She was immaculately dressed in a soft blue and white dress with her hair carefully combed in soft brown waves. She wore a cameo on a band around her neck. Then it was that I met the girl I had seen in church. Her name was Pauline Rhodes. It seemed I had known her all my life. Yet she was a mystery to me. As I have looked back on that occasion, I constantly associated her with Wordsworth's thoughts:

> She was a phantom of delight
> When first she gleamed on my sight;
> A lovely apparition, sent
> To be a moment's ornament;
> Her eyes as stars of twilight fair;
> Like twilight's, too, her dusky hair;
> But all things else about her drawn
> From May-time and the cheerful dawn;
> A dancing shape, an image gay,
> To haunt, to startle, and way-lay.

I was faced with a dilemma: I had always felt it to be both unwise and wrong for a pastor to date members of his church.

No formal dates took place, but I took advantage of being in groups with her, at her home as a guest, and on journeys with her at every chance I got. Much to my amazement, *she* took every discreet chance to be with me. Then we began writing to each other. Then we began meeting each other in Raleigh and Wake Forest. We fell deeply in love with each other. For the first time in my life I did not feel intensely lonely. Pauline understood and accepted me. She could affirm my mother and the rest of my family.

We decided to be married, and I was concerned about the effect this would have on the churches. I asked Mr. Jimmy White, a very wise deacon in the Bunn Church, for his advice. He told me that I would have many churches and, he hoped, one wife. Therefore, I should give my love for Pauline precedence over concern about the church. This I did. However, by the time of our wedding, I had enrolled in Duke Divinity School and had left the Peachtree-Bunn field. I had become a part-time associate pastor at the Grace Baptist Church in Durham, North Carolina. We were married in this church on May 31, 1942.

Pauline and I covenanted to get further education together. She attended classes with me at the seminary. We talked together about the substance of the classwork. Our intense learning together was in a shared enthusiasm for speaking the English language correctly. To this day, the *Shorter Oxford English Dictionary* is by her reading couch, and we check the television personalities' use and abuse of the English language—pronunciation, grammar, etc. Once again, words became thematic in our spiritual journey.

We chose to wait five and a half years before having children. We wanted to have graduate school behind us before we had children. Likewise, we knew that we were very different persons. We consciously chose to get really acquainted with each other as persons before we had children. We had—by the time Bill was born on January 11, 1948, and Charles on May 11, 1953—come to a deeper and deeper awareness of the separate individualities we brought to our relationship. Doing this was not all a smooth, conflict-free process. We are both strong-minded, hard to convince, and proudly independent persons. One thing was for certain—we were and are in this relationship "for the duration." Our vows in marriage were simple but not renegotiable. We both had been abandoned early, and we both are tenderly and unambivalently aware of what threats of abandonment can do to the other. Such threats would push either of us to the edge of the abyss. We have a spoken and, more profoundly, a nonverbal understanding that we will reassure rather than threaten each other. What we have in a marriage of forty years' standing is the end result of a persistent eagerness to reassure each other and oversee each other's nonverbal messages with attentiveness and intense competition to outdo one another in kindness. This is the extent of our competitiveness.

Pauline has effectively dealt with my inherent loneliness to the outside limit of what any marital partner can do. However, she is aware of a kind of loneliness in me that has nothing to do with our marriage. She has conveyed this awareness to me most vividly in the following ways. When I am at home and working in my study, she quietly closes my door for me when the noise level in the rest of the house gets too much. Then there was the occasion when we had seen the play depicting the life of Dylan Thomas, that lonely poet who, like me, felt "double-crossed from his mother's womb." She said: "His deep loneliness makes me think of how you seem to feel much of the time." All I could say was: "Yes!" But I felt genuinely loved and unspeakably understood. She's that kind of person—she can put a whole chapter of a book into one unforgettable sentence.

Our two sons, Bill and Charles, have been allies with me in my struggle with loneliness. Often I think that this loneliness is hereditary because each of them seems as an adult now to carry his particular wistfulness, distance, and the still, sad music of humanity. Our elder son, Bill, is gifted in knowing machines, engineering, and the physical world. He has the memories of nearly two years in the Mekong Delta gunboats of the Riverine Assault Group to remember. Yet his memories seem to be of the Vietnamese people, whom he came to love, more than morbid rumination about the hails of bullets, rockets, and mortar fire he endured safely.

Our younger son, Charles, felt the loneliness of having me preoccupied to distraction about the safety of his brother in the war. He is a physician now; neurology is his specialty. He has lived acutely aware of my neurological problems with a damaged and deteriorating spine. Yet he himself carries his own load of loneliness which comes with the territory of being the physician of catastrophically damaged human beings.

Both these sons' separate disciplines in seeing and participating in the unspeakable tragedy of human life have created among the three of us a quaintly sustaining sense of comradeship. From these quite different but profoundly alike sons I have learned the value and therapeutic power of humor, laughter, and satire to transcend and heal loneliness. We work hard at inventing our own jokes out of live situations. We have never, and I repeat, *never* used humor to ridicule or humiliate each other. In medicine and in combat the humor is often a gallows humor, but, as Bill said of the war, "I would have gone crazy if I could not laugh."

This is not a family history, although the temptation is great to make it so. Rather, I am dealing with the struggle to be free of loneliness. When Pauline and our two sons entered my life, they brought beauty, creativity, and individuality in fellowship and love. Yes. These were and are antidotes to loneliness. But they brought more than that—they brought laughter to my life. Throughout his intriguing book, *The Anatomy of an Illness,* Norman Cousins says that laughter was an important component in his recovery from a life-threatening illness. He quotes Sir William Osler as advising doctors "who are spiritually and physically depleted to find their own medicine in mirth" (Norman Cousins, *The Anatomy of an Illness as Perceived by the Patient,* p. 85; W. W. Norton & Co., 1979).

The laughter my family generates for me has made the end of many days a medicine of mirth.

Laughter is a deeply social experience; it is the antithesis of loneliness. I know people laugh "to themselves," but in reasonably healthy people such laughter is often remembered communion with others. I am not thinking of the laughter of ridicule, disparagement, and cruel jokes when I say that laughter is a social experience. These kinds of laughter are miscarriages of communion. Nevertheless, in themselves they are not asocial but antisocial forms of humor.

As for me, though, my wife and our sons brought laughter into my life. Before them, life had been a solitary and somber pilgrimage of a thoroughly lonely person. The years as a page, as a weaver, as a college student did not teach me laughter. I took everything equally seriously, thus impairing my perspective of what was genuinely important, what should be ignored, what should be shrugged off, and what deserved full attention. In this sense the capacity for laughter is an aid to spiritual discernment, a task not often taken, as it should be, as the primary work of a Christian pastor.

In addition to laughter, Pauline, Bill, and Charles have brought a gentleness into my otherwise ruthlessly tough approach to life. Whatever gentleness I may now have is a grafting of the spirit of Pauline onto mine. Though I hurt to think of times when I have been harsh with her or the children, I give thanks to God for the tenderness they all three have shown me, the extreme rarity of unkind words or acts from them. In the disciplines of psychotherapy and the pastoral arts, I have been able to learn the "oughtness" of steadfast kindness; in my relationship with Pauline, Bill, and Charles I have learned the "isness" of it.

Embracing Loneliness

At the outset of this chapter, I said that the genuinely lonely person not only feels the pain of loneliness but in one sense actually prefers it, embraces it as the price of his or her privacy. Immanuel Kant spoke of the creative functions of the *privatus intellectus,* the private mind. Pauline and I had not been married long until I discovered that she is paradoxically a very social being and at the same time a very private person. To me, therefore, she has always been an intriguingly mysterious being. Her deepest feelings, from prayer to criticism, she has tended to write down rather than say in words. She has an ingrained insistence on maintaining her own interior thoughts.

At first this frustrated and angered a wordy person like me. But on longer and closer view, I have come to reverence it as her own integrity and private relationship to God making itself known. The mystical miracle is, also, that she quietly assumes that I too have an inner world of my own that is not to be "chattered into" with inanities often parading themselves as intimacy, closeness, and "communication." Whatever happens to our marriage, one thing is sure: it will not be "talked into the ground." Nonverbal resonance is its essence. Our deepest prayers are often silent ones, especially as we travel together in the car.

So it is. Such a marriage, though, puts each of us on her or his own before God. This is the crucial aloneness that—if it is to be assuaged—*no* human being can assuage it without trying to be God. Mind you, there is always an abundance of both friends and enemies who readily aspire to demanding your idolatry of them. Turn your life solely over to me, to us, to our organization, to our party, to our institution, to our interpretation of the Bible, to our kind of psychotherapy, and we will give you all of the authority of all the kingdoms of the world which we have just shown you in a moment of time (cf. Luke 4:4-7). This is the way we are lured into the power of all those whose Luciferian demeanor enchants us: we can't stand the loneliness of our own God-given wilderness. We escape from its freedom through believing the promises of the pretenders to God's place in our lives.

Therefore I stubbornly embrace that existential loneliness

which inheres in our humanness. It is not the result of something my parents did to or for—or did not do to or for—me when I was little. I stubbornly resist the fantasy that the perfect woman who meets my every need will erase every tinge of loneliness. I prefer Pauline, who, to quote Wordsworth again, is

> A countenance in which did meet
> Sweet records, promises as sweet;
> A creature not too bright or good
> For human nature's daily food;
> For transient sorrows, simple wiles,
> Praise, blame, love, kisses, tears, and smiles.

I stubbornly resist the theologians, scientists, physicians, gurus, movements, organizations, bureaucracies, etc., who interpret the right to resist and chart my own course, and the privacy of my own thoughts, as disloyalty to their cause. The competency of the human spirit before God and God alone is a prize worth the cost of the loneliness that this stubbornness entails. From its outer side, seen by others, this stubbornness of spirit is never mistaken for humility; yet, walking humbly *with God* calls for it.

Such loneliness is the stuff of which the mystical consciousness of the mysterious tremendousness and the mysterious fascination of our encounter with the Holy is made. Since Moses took his shoes off in this Presence and was made aware of his inability to speak clearly of what was happening to him, this encounter has been the central source of peace, healing, and freedom from the crippling fear of death for anyone who will hazard and embrace the loneliness of being human.

We do all sorts of vain things to numb ourselves to the pain of this hunger for God. We pile up big bibliographies of our writings; we build big and successful organizations; we chase from one set of theories to another; we drink too much booze or do the "in" drug as a sophism; we glorify the visions and revelations of LSD and marijuana; we buy more and more

symbols of affluence; we sit immobilized in inaction waiting for
our big break to come. Yet the yoke of grace and the burden of
unswerving contemplation of the glory of God is a lonely but
renewing responsibility to take upon us (Matt. 11:29). It is here
that loneliness is transformed for me into solitude that enables
me to run and not be weary, to walk and not faint (Isa. 40:31).

Carl Sandburg spoke most eloquently of loneliness in an
interview with Ralph McGill in 1966. He and McGill were
walking about on Glassy Mountain, near Sandburg's home in
North Carolina. Sandburg told McGill: "I often walk here to be
alone. Loneliness is an essential part of a man's life and
sometimes he must seek it out. I sit here and I look out at the
silent hills and I say, 'Who are you, Carl? Where are you going?
What about yourself, Carl?' You know, one of the biggest jobs a
person has is to learn how to live with loneliness. Too many
persons allow loneliness to take them over. It is necessary to
have within oneself the ability to use loneliness. Time is the
coin of life. You spend it. Do not let others spend it for you."

For me, the quality of a certain kind of loneliness necessitates
that fellowship with God which transforms loneliness into
solitude. Augustine spoke of God as "Thou, Almighty, who art
with me, yea, before I am with thee" (*Confessions*, Book X, Sec.
6). I have chosen to be concerned for this *beforeness* in my
vocation as a practical mystic in the maelstrom of events that
flow over my awareness. The act of concern of being alone with
God turns loneliness into solitude, contemplation, and
fellowship with God.

This vocation became apparent to me between my freshman
and sophomore years of college when once again I worked as a
weaver at the Cannon Towel Company to save money to go to
school that fall. A weaver who worked beside me at that time
was an uneducated pastor of a small Baptist congregation on the
outskirts of the mill town. I told him I had decided to be a
minister. He and I covenanted to read the Gospel of John at
nights and discuss it at lunch each day. We learned what the
Fourth Gospel has to say about the specific work of the Holy

Spirit—to be with us that we be not as orphans; to convince us of sin, of righteousness, and of judgment; to bring to our remembrance the things Jesus had taught us; to help Christians to be at one with each other as Christ and the Father are one. Since that time I have practiced the presence of the Spirit as my Counselor and Teacher alongside me.

In my junior year of college I lived in the home of a family who were Quakers. They invited me to their Quaker meetings. The silence, the dependence upon the inner light of the Spirit, the search for an "agreed oneness in decision-making" pushed my mystical search farther on its way. I read the works of Rufus Jones, especially his book *The Church's Debt to Its Heretics*.

While in college and seminary also, through Olin Binkley I met Joel Rufus Moseley, a Baptist mystic who wrote a remarkably influential book, *Manifest Victory*. He led groups of students in voluntary spiritual seekers groups when he visited our campuses. I drank deeply at the Pierian spring of wisdom, humor, spiritual commitment, and freedom of spirit that was Rufus Moseley. Here again the mystical way of Christ spoke to my loneliness, turning it into solitude and contemplation.

This spiritual concern was enhanced by the privilege of serving as an adjunct professor at Earlham School of Religion in Richmond, Indiana, for several years. I learned a fresh new component for pastoral counseling and psychotherapy as I conversed with students and faculty there. The intentional practice of the disciplines of peace and the search for the life of the Spirit in the process of theological education became a wholehearted commitment of mine to teaching small numbers of students. This commitment had much to do with my leaving the large classes of the Southern Baptist Theological Seminary—loving them though I did—to take a position at the University of Louisville School of Medicine, where my teaching work is on a small-group and one-to-one basis.

Meditation has become a very popular and trendy thing today. I do not find myself at home with these emphases, though I do not mean to disparage them. I am for any reasonable thing that will slow Americans down for as much as twenty minutes a day. (Maybe suddenly turning all traffic lights red at the same time for twenty minutes a day would help. The logistics of *how* to do that are impossible.)

In the face of this concern for the practice of the presence of the Spirit, I wrote my small book *Nurturing Silence in a Noisy Heart* (1979). It reflects much of my struggle to be free of loneliness. Yet the central issue is that we are not only made for community; at base, as Augustine said, we are made by God for fellowship with God, and our hearts are restless until we find that fellowship with God.

The Comradeship of the Holy Spirit: An Invitation to Dialogue

Your loneliness is of intense importance to me, not just my loneliness. These pages are the outreach from my own loneliness to you in yours. That's one great reason we write anything—to transcend our own loneliness and to connect with our readers' loneliness. You may look for the ultimate answer to your loneliness in some *one* other human being—a parent, a son or daughter, a spouse, a friend of the same or the opposite sex. As others find this ultimate demand being laid upon them, they probably withdraw from you or fall into conflict with you, at best, or reject you outright for being too possessive, consuming, and even jealous of them. No human being's frailty can stand this kind of omnivorous loneliness that literally eats one up.

Or again, you may simply assume that the *only* assuagement of loneliness is other people and become a joiner of groups, clubs, and other such companies of people. Instead of this, you may go in the opposite direction and devote your life to "wailing." It is not by chance that in Jerusalem there is a Wailing Wall where Jews gather on Fridays to pray and lament. In our country, we have no such ritualization of wailing. Yet you may be a wailing person of one kind or another. In either event—to immerse yourself in groups as a joiner or to spend your life wailing—you are in different ways saying: "I am orphaned, desolate, alone." You are saying, as the Ancient Mariner did:

> Alone, alone, all, all alone,
> Alone on a wide wide sea!
> And never a saint took pity on
> My soul in agony.

I have the choice and you have the choice as to whether we make this the controlling motif of our lives. The creation story says that we are not meant to be alone. We are to have partners who are equal, responsive, and considerate of us and we of them (Gen. 2:18), even though we are different from each other. As I learned in studying the Gospel of John with my fellow mill worker, Jesus promised that he would not leave us as orphans, desolate. He promised: "If a man loves me, he will keep my word, and my Father will love him, and we will come to him and make our home with him." The gift of this *home* is the solid assurance that we neither are alone nor need *feel* alone. He is with us always (Matt. 28:20).

This Presence is unconditionally *here*. We need not stand gazing into the sky waiting for him nor wallow in self-pity as we wail. This Presence shapes our feelings, if we permit it, but is never driven away by our feelings, whatever they may be. This Presence is the Presence of a God who has a sense of humor and aims to keep us in good enough humor, as the hymn "I Would Be True" puts it, to "laugh, and love, and lift." Just when life has become thoroughly absurd, we are given the gift of laughter that says, "This is ridiculous!" and follows it with, "This too will pass away," and completes it with, "I will never leave nor forsake you!" Consequently, as we cultivate the presence of the One who has made his home with us, we can say with the apostle Paul: "We are afflicted in every way, but not crushed; perplexed, but not driven to despair; persecuted, but not forsaken; struck down, but not destroyed; always carrying in the body the death of Jesus, so that the life of Jesus may also be manifested in our bodies" (II Cor. 4:8-10). Hence you and I do not rush pell-mell into groups or crowds. Nor do we spend our lives wailing, "Pity me." We have a home in God through Jesus Christ here and now. We have a vocation to permit the life of Jesus Christ to be made manifest in all our doings, goings, comings, and thinkings so that we are not in this all by ourselves.

5
To Be Free
from Factory Education

WHEN I STARTED public school in 1923 there were only half as many people in the United States as there are now. Transportation and communication were relatively undeveloped, so that it was common for a neighborhood school to be a face-to-face community of people who knew and lived near each other. The teacher in a community such as ours, where the average educational level was about the sixth grade, was a highly respected person. Teachers earned a salary better than that of most people whose children they taught. Yet the poverty and ignorance around them made them somehow "missionaries" to us. They valued and esteemed their positions and guarded with great care the examples they set before us.

Only until my own sons entered public school, and especially now that our two grandchildren have entered the same system, did I realize how dramatically the situation of the teacher and the public school had deteriorated from what I knew as a child and youth.

Let me ask you: "Do you find yourself in quiet—and sometimes not so quiet—despair about the overcrowded classrooms, the lack of individual attention to children's needs, and the politicization of the educational system?" Well, I find myself perplexed, concerned, and many times angry about what David Elkind, a noted psychologist at Tufts University, calls "factory education." He has written a remarkable book, *The Hurried Child* (Addison-Wesley Publishing Co., 1981), in which he says: "For the moment, the factory management systems in education seem to be the most prevalent, and consequently children are being pressured to produce for the sake of teachers and administrators."

As I read this comment, I was filled with awe, wonder, and gratitude that I, a street kid from the mill villages of the Carolinas, received a very personalized, individually tailored, and custom-made education in my formative, collegiate, and graduate years. My entry into the teaching profession as a minister was made with nonfactory conditions and presuppositions in mind. However, much, but not all, of the theological education into which I entered *has* been that of the factory-management kind. Therefore, my whole teaching career has been a struggle for freedom for myself and my students from the destructive and deadening effects of that factory-education approach. As I raise this subject with you, let me say that my struggle as an adult to be free of factory education is an important part of my life history.

Let me consider with you my seminary education. I took the first year of my seminary training at Duke Divinity School. I took a full year of Old Testament under Professor Stinespring, a full year of New Testament under Professor Clark, a full year of advanced Greek under Professor Branscomb, and a full year of church history under Professor Petry. They took considerable care to push me forward to courses that more nearly fitted my level of preparation after my work at Wake Forest College. This was at their initiative and with no expectation on my part. They used a custom-built approach to curriculum. The classes were small because there were few men who had not been drafted into the military service. I volunteered as a Navy chaplain, but my crooked arm from the fight as a page, a missing finger due to a mislick with a hatchet at a woodpile at the hands of my next oldest brother, and a history of a kidney stone flunked me on the physical.

My time at Duke was creatively spent. I grew by leaps and bounds. They taught me to use *primary* sources, i.e., to read

Clement of Alexandria, Francis of Assisi, et al., themselves, and to use but little time reading *about* them. This we did. The Duke University library, cross-referenced with that of the University of North Carolina, was an outstanding organization, one of the most efficient libraries in which I have ever worked.

All of this academic excellence was balanced by my pastoral work under the supervision of Rev. Henry B. Anderson, a consistent model of a man who taught intuitively using Biblical language, and who worked incessantly in the personal pastoral care of his people. Little wonder that Pauline and I grieved when we packed all our goods into a 1935 Ford and headed over the mountains to Louisville, Kentucky, to take up our second year of seminary work at the Southern Baptist Theological Seminary in July 1943.

I met with cultural shock upon arrival at the school. Whereas I was given every personal consideration by faculty and staff outside the classroom, I found the school to be woefully understaffed. The school had barely emerged from the Great Depression. The war was at its fiercest pitch. The policy had been to make do with the faculty they had rather than to add new members. Attrition by death had taken one or two faculty members; old age and retirement had taken two more; resignation had taken two more. Another was severely handicapped and in failing health. The remaining members of a fine faculty were severely overworked. Funds were scarce and salaries were low. Even as an entering middler, I had the acumen to count this into my assessment of the nature and quality of instruction. From this point forward, do not let my critique of the educational situation obscure my profound affection for this school.

The classes were larger by four or five times than any classes I had ever attended. The professors rarely lectured or led in discussion. They assigned sections of books to be read, outlined, and memorized. The classroom time was spent in calling on different students to recite from memory the material that had been assigned. Also, "pop quizzes" were given for recounting the material. We were not asked to do research on our own. Our own capacity to interpret data was not exercised and critiqued.

The curriculum was the same for all students. There were only two electives, one in the philosophy of religion and one in the psychology of religion.

The redeeming grace of the teaching methodology and curriculum at that time was that no one was assumed to know, or had it taken for granted that he knew, what the Bible said. Students were required to know the subject matter from memory. This meant the Hebrew, the Greek, and the English Bible. How long one remembered all this is another question, but he had to remember it at least until the next recitation or quiz. I remember the Bible because I *had* to know it, and I am grateful for the nondebatable discipline that caused the Bible to become a part of my natural speech.

During 1943–44, there were 596 students at the Southern Baptist Theological Seminary. I was in classes of over a hundred in most instances. The papers we wrote on examinations were read by "fellows" or teaching assistants who also taught the class when the professor was absent. I recall the disappointment I felt when I wrote a paper on "Jesus' Experience of the Holy Spirit in the Synoptic Gospels." The paper was returned with an "A" but no commentary as to whether my exegesis could be improved. This cut me off from dialogue with another mind as informed as, or better informed than, mine on the subject. Furthermore, for the first time in my life I found myself in "factory education," as Elkind defines it. I was lucky to have avoided it that long.

As I look back now, I am awed that I could have had such an intensely personalized education throughout my life until I was twenty-six years of age! I began to search on the ground on which I was standing to see if I could find anyone who could continue this kind of education. I found faculty members yearning for this custom approach to teaching. They were heroically making the best of a tough situation.

In the classrooms of some professors I found something different. Particularly was this true of Gaines S. Dobbins, who taught church administration and psychology of religion. In the course in psychology of religion (which only forty people took!) he put us to work on experimental projects. He arranged with Spafford Ackerly, M.D., professor of psychiatry at the Louisville University School of Medicine and Louisville General Hospital, for a group of us to serve as psychiatric aides in return for lectures and discussions on the pathology of religious experience.

In my senior year, he asked me to direct a new group of twenty-one students in this project. This was my small path to personalized education. Dr. Dobbins seemed to have no limit to the personal time he gave our group. He and Dr. Ackerly both were personal friends of Dr. Anton Boisen, author of *The Exploration of the Inner World; Religion in Crisis and Custom;* and *Problems in Religion and Life*. They introduced our group to Boisen, a lonely, intrepid explorer of the inner world. He was filled with a concern for the "Love which would surmount every barrier, and bridge every chasm, and make sure the foundations of the universe" (dedication page of *The Exploration of the Inner World;* Willett, Clark & Co., 1936). This man presented us with a radical departure in education for any profession. He called it "clinical training of pastors." He saw it as a small-group study of the "living human documents" of persons in dire circumstances at the edge of the abyss between self-discovery and the destructive forces of the nethermost regions of suffering. His phrase "the living human documents" has become the hallmark phrase for this hand-tooled, custom-crafted form of education. His approach was the antithesis of "factory education." His concern was to join in the struggles of people for deliverance from the power of the law and of sin into the redemption Jesus Christ has to offer. Redemption was not a matter of joining some organization, but of being delivered out of the jaws of death and destruction into life and creativity. This man had been there. He endured three psychotic episodes before he was fifty-nine and recovered to function well each time. He lived to tell his story, to start the clinical pastoral training movement, and to leave a large number of empirical studies of cases and groups of cases in peer-refereed medical and psychiatric journals

I took my first quarter of clinical pastoral training with Chaplain Ralph Bonacker at the Norton Memorial Infirmary. He was an Episcopal pastor. He was theologically attuned and psychoanalytically trained. He insisted that we lead morning prayers in the chapel daily. He pushed us for a personal grasp of the theological roots of the problems of patients and of our own personal histories. We ourselves were taken as living human documents and pushed to read with understanding what had been written thus far. For example, the relentless clutch of the habitual ways of doing were spoken of psychoanalytically as the superego. The same realities were spoken of by Paul as "the law." Both were the "spirit of bondage" from which Christ had come to deliver us, sending the Holy Spirit to empower us to cast off the yoke of bondage. This is the way Ralph Bonacker taught—simply, directly, clearly, and personally.

I continued to work under Bonacker's supervision for the academic year 1944–45. We had a group of students who worked twelve hours a week for thirty-six weeks in an extended quarter during the academic year, all the while taking a full load of classes at the seminary. Dr. Dobbins met with us one evening a week and thereby enabled us to get academic credit for the work. These were the beginnings of a whole new elective curriculum at the Southern Baptist Theological Seminary. It was a creative alternative to "factory education."

In the summer of 1945, I went to Elgin State Hospital at Elgin, Illinois, where Dr. Anton Boisen was chaplain, to take a third quarter of clinical pastoral education with him. When Pauline and I arrived, we learned that the Northeastern-Midwestern organization known as the Council for Clinical Training had, for reasons still unclear to me, invalidated Dr. Boisen as a supervisor and installed another person who was much less informed, experienced, and capable in his place. However, Dr. Boisen remained as chaplain of the hospital; in fact, however, I think he was not paid as chaplain. He was called chaplain emeritus, or some such title. The fact that he was there kept us there. Otherwise we would have left. I was appalled by the slavish acceptance of a watered-down, poorly researched Freudianism being taught by the formal supervisor. I was amazed at his rule that in the seminars we could not discuss theology or the religious beliefs of patients until the last week of the twelve-week unit.

I was getting ready to take an instructorship in a theological school. I was searching for a way to introduce the clinical approach into the context of a seminary curriculum. The separation of theology from the day-to-day work until the last week would never work there. Nor was this the way of Boisen or of Bonacker. I rejected it.

By the time I left this group I was convinced that both Freud and the Christian faith had been badly served. I sustained my relationship with Dr. Boisen but was distinctly committed to the integration of clinical pastoral training into the curriculum, and not treating it as a separate operation, as I perceived the Council for Clinical Training to be doing. Their independence of seminaries meant maybe too much to them.

I returned to Louisville to begin my first year of graduate work at the Baptist Seminary. I already had an appointment as an instructor in psychology of religion. I continued a fourth extended-quarter group with Ralph Bonacker that fall and winter. Bonacker and I continued to work together with much harmony, despite the fact that he told me that I was negatively perceived by the director of the Council for Clinical Training. This negative reaction would appear later.

Concurrently with returning to the seminary, I had been appointed as an instructor at the seminary and as a part-time chaplain at Kentucky Baptist Hospital. I made $1,200 a year at the seminary and $1,000 a year at the hospital! I taught a class in the night school of the University of Louisville for $600 a semester. But Pauline did not have to work, and we both stayed in school. We looked forward to doughnuts on Sunday evenings or a trip to a cafeteria downtown for recreation!

Work with Bonacker continued with excellent results throughout 1945–46. In the spring, I began to plan for a group of students of my own at the Kentucky Baptist Hospital. I wanted to supervise five students myself and have Bonacker supervise my supervision. Thus they could be certified by the Council for Clinical Training, and I would be on my way to becoming a supervisor.

For this, Bonacker said, I would need the approval of the director of the Council for Clinical Training. I went to Elgin to see the director. I presented my case to him, but he said that he could not approve me as a supervisor because I had been so negative with him and the other supervisor the summer before. I did not debate the matter with him nor beg him to accept me. I simply said that this let me know firsthand where I stood with him and where he stood with me. Once again, I was being muscled into pack thinking with persons whose approach to clinical pastoral training I considered would never work at Southern Baptist Seminary.

I returned to Louisville, conferred with Dr. Dobbins, with the superintendent of Kentucky Baptist Hospital, H. L. Dobbs, and with the president of the seminary, Dr. Ellis A. Fuller. All three agreed that the thing to do was to start our own local program of clinical pastoral education without any need for alliance with the Council for Clinical Training. Our decision was to integrate the work into the curriculum of the Southern Baptist Theological Seminary and to make the leadership of the program completely answerable academically to the faculty of the seminary and clinically to the medical staff and administration of the hospitals where we worked.

This was a break with the Council for Clinical Training before a real relationship had begun. My point of view about the clinical method of theological and pastoral enquiry was then, has been since, and is today, that which Anton Boisen conveyed to me in a handwritten letter of June 18, 1946: "As I see it the function of the Council is far less to determine and enforce standards than [it is] to make possible collaboration on the part of those who are working in this field for the furtherance of their common objectives." In my words, our objective was to create a fellowship of clinically-minded persons and not to create a board of control for certification. It pointed up my basic difference with the council at the point of gaining academic stature for the discipline in the context of theological education. It was a breakthrough at the seminary, because it was a custom-made rather than a mass-production kind of education. It was made an approved part of the curriculum, at least formally. For it to become vitally so, affecting the whole fabric of the curriculum, would require a struggle only dimly perceived by both myself and the faculty as a whole. To the majority of the faculty I was significant only insofar as I was competent in their classes and by reason of my being an instructor in the department of which Dr. Gaines Dobbins was chairman. One person, Olin Binkley, besides Dr. Dobbins, perceived the educational departure inherent in what I was doing. It was *not* factory education. Both shared my struggle to be free of mass-production approaches to education.

However, the director of the Council for Clinical Training mailed special delivery, registered letters to President Fuller and H. L. Dobbs of Kentucky Baptist Hospital seeking to abort the work I had started by telling them that it did not have the council's approval. They in turn conferred with me and wrote courteous letters saying that my work had all the approval required by them. From then on, as far as my function with the council was concerned, the whole matter was a closed book.

After all this, a much tougher struggle ensued: establishing the custom-made clinical approach to theological education *within* the very heart of theological curricula. That task made other struggles seem trivial by comparison. But I was committed to do so. I knew what the issue was from the beginning: the struggle to be free and to free students from factory education.

In the spring of 1948, I was elected to the faculty of the Southern Baptist Theological Seminary as an assistant professor of psychology of religion, after having served two years as a graduate student instructor. I faced the formidable task of developing a curriculum, a leadership, and a body of literature for a field that was as yet unmined ore. Harold Tribble, professor of theology; Olin Binkley, professor of Christian ethics; Sydnor Stealey, professor of church history; and Gaines Dobbins, professor of church administration, had been my doctoral committee. They were veteran pastors and teachers. They knew about the power plays within faculties, particularly this one. They knew that power struggles were very personal, and not ethereal, philosophical struggles of ideas. I later heard Daniel Day Williams of Union Theological Seminary wisely observe that any school curriculum represents not necessarily what students most need in their education, but the prevailing power balance in the faculty and administration at the time. He was referring to all institutions of higher education and not just the one where I worked then or now. The senior professors provided me with the cautions, wisdom, strategies, and support for devising a curriculum that would get the approval of the whole faculty. They were far more accepting of me as a hostile-aggressive person than any clinical training persons I had encountered except Bonacker.

I was naive. I thought *all* the revered older men on the faculty had my best interest at heart! Some of them had only their own interest at heart instead! It took three majority approving votes of the faculty over a period of a year to get the clinical pastoral education units defined as elective credit courses into the catalog for students to read. I finally discovered that the secretary of the faculty was simply not recording the votes. On the third round, I made copies for everyone, filed them with the president's secretary, and went with the faculty member who was the "minutes keeper" to see that he wrote it into the minutes! He really was opposed to the whole process!

The courses became immediately popular. The fond dream of custom-woven education was a victim of its own success. The intensive, personal, action-centered clinical programs were restricted to ten people in a group. As we developed more supervisors, such as Lyn Elder at Kentucky Baptist Hospital, Everett Barnard at Missouri Baptist Hospital in St. Louis, Aaron Rutledge at Central State Hospital in Louisville, and Richard Young at North Carolina Baptist Hospitals in Winston-Salem, the pressure eased as some of the demands were met.

However, I learned that if the program was to have students who had an information background to take into the intensive groups, then larger lecture classes with small-group assignments could be helpful, though this was a partial capitulation to the factory-education approach. Therefore, I began to lecture in courses on the work of the Christian pastor, psychology of religion, religious dimensions of personality, and marriage and family counseling. I discovered that my public speaking skills, my capacity to capture an audience with the dramas of pastoral work, and my ability to write blended together. Out of these class lectures began coming my books, beginning with *The Christian Pastor*, published in 1951. (The third edition, revised, of this book was published in 1982.) I saw my task enlarging to include producing a literature in the field. I consulted closely with Paul Johnson of Boston University School of Theology about curriculum and literature. I met Seward Hiltner of the National Council of Churches and later of the University of Chicago through my first efforts at writing an article entitled "The Role of Religion in the Psychoses." He became my lifelong friend, consultant, and collaborator in producing a credible and coherent literature. I saw that compromising with the prevailing mode of factory education could be done with integrity in the following ways. First, the subject matter could be defined in textbooks, and the classroom could be used for demonstrations of clinical procedures, collaboration with guest physicians, social workers, psychologists, lawyers, etc. We were able to bring a few counselees into the classroom for dialogue with the class. Members of Alcoholics Anonymous were exceptionally helpful.

Second, we could use the students' own personal experiences with multiple problems and illnesses in themselves or in family members. Routinely, we asked persons to write their own biographies, and to do "time and motion" studies of their varied pastoral tasks. We organized them into verbatim case report study groups and asked graduate students who were in study group dynamics to be their "lab" supervisors. I regularly read their research papers myself. We arranged occasional field trips, but these were not often because of the unwieldy numbers of people, transportation, scheduling, etc.

Third, I kept the morale of the class at a cohesive level by working intensively on fresh, new lecture material presented in unique ways. I got to know the students personally and became aware of their own needs for pastoral attention. I was never able to do this at the level I wanted, because there was not the time or energy to do so. Nevertheless, I was able to do this to such an extent that I could create something of the aura of an intense, personal relationship to each student. This was sweat-producing, concentrated labor, and yet it was deeply satisfying work. Behind the whole effort was my prayer that God forbid that I should allow the overwhelming numbers to turn my teaching into another "factory."

All of my efforts with bachelor of divinity students were, nevertheless, like sweeping back the ocean with a broom. I confessed this to a class one day. The next class period one of them had placed a big push broom at the side of the professor's desk. As I entered the class, a roar of laughter (which was plenteous in these classes) greeted me. I looked at the broom carefully, took it up and used it in the open area, and then remarked: "You have heard it said by them of old that teaching at this institution is like sweeping the ocean back with a broom. But I say unto you, 'I never thought the corporation would furnish the broom.' Thank you!" Yet as the years have passed, I have been amazed to see the specific changes wrought in students' pastoral identity in these large lecture classes.

In order to stay in touch with my ideals of teaching, I discovered that the master of theology degree, which consisted of one full year of classwork and a thesis beyond the bachelor of divinity, was a much-neglected degree. I used this degree for several years as a way of custom-teaching a group of ten students a year. This proved to be a nationally recognized program in 1955, as described in *The Advancement of Theological Education,* by H. Richard Niebuhr, Daniel Day Williams, and James M. Gustafson (Harper & Brothers, 1957):

> The development of the field of pastoral theology at Southern Baptist Seminary in Louisville, Kentucky, illustrates the variety of possibilities which are open and some methods of relating this work to the theological curriculum.
>
> In this school the work in pastoral theology which includes field training in clinical situations is given for the most part at the Th.M. level, after the completion of the B.D. course. The degree is given in theology, not in pastoral counseling. The course is designed to make explicit the relationship between pastoral work and the "body of divinity." Further, the program is kept under the full supervision of the seminary. This means that the institutions in which students work are located in the surrounding geographical area. . . .
>
> The stress placed here upon the relating of studies in pastoral theology to the remainder of the curriculum is characteristic of most of the advanced work being done in this field. The theological perspective is emphasized, and the insights derived from clinical study play their part in the interpretation of the Bible, church history, and theology. (Pp. 126f.)

These Th.M. students have developed in a variety of directions. Two thirds of them are pastors of churches among six or seven different denominations. Several of them—for example, David Edens, Howard Hovde, and Wallace Denton—went to Columbia University Teachers College to complete doctorates in family life development, education, and therapy. Denton and Edens did clinical internships in family therapy at Merrill-Palmer in Detroit under Aaron Rutledge, who had earlier received his doctorate in our program.

The point at which the whole endeavor was justified for me was in the supervision of Ph.D. candidates. Beginning in 1947, working alongside Gaines Dobbins as my mentor, I began to learn the hazards and hopes of graduate supervision. The Ph.D. program itself was overcrowded in the late 1930s and through the 1950s. A great deal of first-class work was done by enterprising and innovative students. Among them were Clarence Jordan of Koinonia Farm in Americus, Georgia, translator of *The Cotton Patch Version* of the New Testament; Carlyle Marney, accomplished preacher, author of many books, and leader of Interpreter's House in Lake Junaluska, North Carolina, for the rehabilitation of burnt-out ministers; and Robert Bratcher, the translator of the New Testament of the *Good News Bible*. But the size of the graduate program was unwieldy, and patterns of supervision were uneven. Standards of excellence varied drastically from department to department. The size of the faculty for offering Ph.D. work was incredibly small in contrast to the number of students. Students often worked full-time at distant places, thus using more time traveling than in study.

These conditions were not and are not today unique to the Southern Baptist Theological Seminary. I found them at Columbia University when teaching at Union Theological Seminary in New York. I have found them in major universities all over the country, including the school where I now work.

Over a period of ten years—from 1958 to 1968—the faculty at Southern Baptist Seminary remedied many of these flaws. A student had to finish his or her work in four years at least or pay heavy fee penalties; he or she had to complete the dissertation while in residence; if illness, financial crisis, bereavement, or family problems occurred, the student was urged or required to take an "interrupted status" until he or she could give primary attention to the graduate program; the dissertation had to be presented to the committee of instruction *unbound* for any changes required after its oral defense, etc.

The faculty, in turn, were required to limit the number of persons under their supervision to five. This rule was the most difficult to maintain, but it was adhered to strictly and served a great disciplinary purpose. Furthermore, when a professor went away on leave or sabbatical, he was required to make arrangements for another professor to replace him. He was not permitted to supervise *in absentia*.

In addition, extensive work was done in building a research-oriented collection in the library. The amount of money invested in books, journals, and completing primary source references was increased exponentially.

These changes produced a much, much smaller body of graduate students. Dissertations began to be of publishable quality; graduates began to find fulfilling work more easily.

These conditions held steady until 1972, when our school was cited by the American Council on Education as one of the three or four best places for graduate work in theological studies. At last we had a handcrafted approach to graduate work. I found great satisfaction in seeing a long sought after dream come into actual being.

However, this satisfaction was short-lived. The economy began to reel, and funds were harder and harder to get. At the same time, the American Association of Theological Schools proposed a new doctor's degree, known as the doctor of ministry degree. The plan was to allow active pastors to commute back and forth to the campus for minimal periods of residence, take courses, get a "crash course" introduction to field research, return to their field of work with a nearby pastor to supervise them, do field study, and write a field project. In my opinion, this was an attempt to mass-produce the field approach that Boisen had pioneered on a handcrafted basis.

Immediately this degree was embraced by the administrations of seminaries all over the United States and handed to their faculties to implement. Faculties were already sorely overloaded as it was. Few of them had had any training in anything but historical, linguistic, and literary methods of research. Social research and field research were a closed book to the majority of theological professors. Some denominations, such as the Lutheran groups, already had a vicarship—a year in supervised praxis between the junior and senior years of seminary. Others had hard-nosed social researchers in charge of the degree. These have developed programs of exceptional quality. However, they have highly limited numbers, also. These avoid the factory-education degree approach to the D.Min. Yet many schools have inordinately large numbers of poorly supervised D.Min. students.

I have had some very positive experiences supervising D.Min. students from both of the major seminaries in our city. My first students were a group of three chaplains in our area, two Fort Knox chaplains and the senior chaplain at University Hospital. However, I insisted, while at the Baptist Seminary, that these people be nearby in residence for two years, insofar as possible.

I felt that the D.Min. degree reflected a great deal of idealism on the part of the American Association of Theological Schools staff. However, the methods of research and types of supervision called for are simply not present in theological faculties. The methods of research in which 95 percent of theological faculties are disciplined are linguistic methods, literary criticism methods, historical survey methods, and hermeneutical methods. Social surveys, case-history methods, and general social research methods are known to an increasing minority. These are the methods apropos of the D.Min. degree.

In the school where I was working at the time, the applications for the degree deluged us. In our school, as in others, the extra financial gain for offering this degree came at the upsurge of the severe inflation of the 1970s.

This demand was compounded in my case in 1972 by the retirement of one of my two colleagues, Dr. D. Swan Haworth. He was not to be replaced. We were expected—my other colleague, Dr. John Boyle, and I—to absorb the load I myself had a set of deep needs to be met that called for a more specialized and intensive teaching load.

In the face of the increasing enrollment at both the M. Div. and graduate levels, my natural curiosity generated a fresh alternative. I sought to negotiate with the administration a new covenant for my duties in which I would be a research professor, carrying a full load of teaching of advanced and graduate classes. To ask this was to ask for a luxury the school by tradition could not afford without making special concessions to me that amounted to favoritism. In the final analysis, the request I made was granted, but after testing the climate of the administration and faculty, I decided that it would not be wise to receive given privileges that every other professor would not have. Furthermore, I had a heavy writing program outlined for the next several years, no personal secretarial help, and few other logistical resources for doing the writing I have done since. I thought at first I could solve these problems by going to Southeastern Baptist Seminary in North Carolina. I resigned and accepted a position there. However, upon closer view, the retirement of their president, Olin T. Binkley, my esteemed mentor for thirty-seven years, occasioned an unstable situation that I could not in all good faith enter. Therefore, I decided not to go there. Nevertheless, I was committed to finding a place where I could teach, do research, and write on a personal and not a mass-production basis.

These were anxious days but very exhilarating ones. I had often quoted lines from Minnie Louise Haskins' poem, beginning:

> And I said to the man who stood at the gate of the year:
> "Give me a light, that I may tread safely into the
> unknown!"

I had quoted it. Now I was in a position of taking my own advice. So, putting my hand into the hand of God, I stepped out into the unknown.

As I look back now, I can empathize with the administrations of big schools. I had asked for a luxury that few can afford. Though the privilege was granted, if I had accepted it, the privations of the rest of the faculty would have become painfully evident, because they too were overloaded. The economic issues for which school administrators are responsible stagger the mind to consider. The compromises and presumptions upon their faculties and students into which raw economic problems push them are compelling. Yet throughout the American educational system the commitment to a custom-made, highly personal professor-student alliance in learning has a very, very low priority. Some austerity at all other points and a focus of resources at this point would improve the problems of finance and support of schools, especially in theological schools. Yet, for myself, I was committed to an intense personal austerity, if need be, to bring into being a quality level of education of a custom-made kind to the discipline of teaching. Where and how it would happen for me at the age of fifty-seven, God only knew. Whatever it cost to make it happen, Pauline and I were ready to pay. We were never more closely bonded than in this decision.

Within three months of my resignation from the Southeastern Seminary offer, I had the opportunity to see my struggle for freedom to do intensive personal teaching rewarded. My esteemed colleague and friend—indeed, my brother in Christ—Leslie Van Nostrand, M.D., called me one evening to discuss my work plans with me. Since 1949 I had been a theological consultant for the Department of Psychiatry of the University of Louisville School of Medicine. Leslie said that he had talked with Professor and Chairman John Schwab, M.D., of the Department of Psychiatry and Behavioral Sciences. He had urged him to bring me into the faculty of the School of Medicine as a specialist in the psychopathology of religion and pastoral counseling. He *told* me to send Dr. Schwab my curriculum vitae and to call his secretary for an appointment with him. I did so and met with Dr. Schwab in early April. We talked leisurely and in depth. He told me of his heritage as a mountaineer from East Kentucky. I told him of my heritage. We discussed the foci of interests evident in my curriculum vitae. Then he asked me a penetrating question: "Are you acquainted with Louisville General Hospital?" I told him that that was where I had started in this field and that I had been in almost weekly interaction with the hospital since 1944. He had already conferred with Dr. Ackerly and Dr. William Keller, the former chairman of the department. He had closely collaborated with E. E. Landis, M.D., another senior member of the faculty, who had been my teacher, friend, and confidant since 1948. He said: "A tidal wave of the human suffering of poor people comes in there regularly. That is where I would want you to spend most of your time." Then he said to me: "We want you to come aboard as a full professor with tenure to be granted after one year, according to policy." We agreed upon a salary and he said, "I will find the money." On July 1, 1974, I joined the University of Louisville faculty. On July 30, 1974, my tenure at Southern Baptist Theological Seminary ended.

The educational system of a medical school is drastically different from that of a theological school. The "preclinical" freshman and sophomore years are really a mill of the gods that grinds exceedingly fine. Students must be expert at taking machine-scored, multiple-choice question tests. They have mountains of minuscule data to master. As one of them said: "It is not all that difficult; it's all that much." At this point, factory education is in full swing. In the clinical clerkships, the senior tutorials, and the psychiatric residency, the teaching-supervision and learning is highly personalized and the mentor-protégé relationship has full expression. When I add to these teaching relationships the small groups of pastoral counseling residents who come to me from seminaries near and far, I have the best of both worlds in medical and theological education.

For me, at least, factory education is, I pray, a thing of my past.

In my present work about 96 percent of my teaching is free of the bondage to factory education. It came to me not as the result of a struggle but as a gift of the grace of God and the spiritual sensitivity and willingness to take a risk by employing me on the part of Drs. John Schwab, E. E. Landis, Spafford Ackerly, and Billie Keller, Dean Arthur Keeney, President James Grier Miller, and Dr. Leslie Van Nostrand. They expect me to exercise my expertise as a pastor, theologian, and pastoral counselor. They expect me to do so without apology. It is a sheer luxury to be able to know each of my resident colleagues in depth and personally, as well as to be known the same way by them.

The protégé-mentor modality for teaching and learning is badly needed in our schools today. On or about August 23 of this year our little grandson, Will, starts to kindergarten. His sister, Shannon, has already been badly mauled by an inept school system. I wonder whether he will be able to find teachers who see it as a part of their job to relate to him as an individual person. Will he have to learn how to "finesse" the system to get grades, to get a good report card, to get a diploma, to get the right to ask for a job? Or will he learn because he knows his teacher, his teacher knows him, and they *care* about learning as one of the greatest adventures of life? As Jerome Bruner suggests, learning is generated by "an attitude toward learning and inquiry, toward guessing and hunches, toward the possibility of solving problems on one's own. The important ingredient in such learning is a sense of excitement about discovery—discovery of regularities of previously unrecognized relations and similarities between ideas, with a resulting sense of self-confidence in one's abilities" (*The Process of Education*, p. 20; Harvard University Press, 1960). I would prefer, pray for, and be willing to pay for this—and would defy death to live a little longer to see this happen. He is not a statistic, existing to assure so many dollars to the budgeted income of a school. He is not a commodity to be counted, not raw material to be made to fit factory specifications. He is a boy named Will. He has a mind of his own that can observe itself, decide its own destiny, and go its own particular way. This boy, like other children, is, as Norman Cousins puts it well, no mere child: "Moral splendor comes with the gift of life." He "has the capacity for identification, dedication, sacrifice, and mutuality." He "has unlimited strength to feel human oneness and to act upon it. The tragedy of life is not in the fact of death but what dies inside of us while we live" (*Human Options: An Autobiographical Notebook*, p. 45; W. W. Norton & Co., 1981). My passion for something better than, other than, and different from factory education for Will and Shannon is still very much alive and well. And Will and Shannon are for me archetypal representatives of every child that goes forth to learn. As Walt Whitman wrote in his *Leaves of Grass:*

> There was a child went forth every day,
> And the first object he look'd upon, that object he became,
> And that object became part of him for the day or a certain part of the day,
> Or for many years or stretching cycles of years.
>
> .   .   .   .
>
> His own parents, he that had father'd him and she that had conceived him in her womb and birth'd him,
> They gave this child more of themselves than that,
> They gave him afterward every day, they became part of him.
>
> .   .   .   .
>
> These became part of that child who went forth every day,
> and who now goes, and will always go forth every day.

Jesus, the Teacher Come from God, and His Students (Disciples): An Invitation to Dialogue

Nicodemus said to Jesus that he knew Jesus was "a teacher come from God." His ministry showed that God was with him (John 3:2). You and I hunger for this kind of instruction for ourselves and our children, and our children's children. The heart of that teaching was the powerful relationship Jesus established personally with his students. Furthermore, intense commitment on their part was required. Obedience to his word, manner of being, and way of life, he promised them, would enable them to know the truth, and the truth would make them free (John 8:31-32).

Furthermore, Jesus, in teaching his disciples, did not promise them learning without a struggle. Teaching and learning to him were not a matter of passing or failing courses. They were concerned with matters of life and death, probably his disciples' own death and certainly Jesus' death on the cross. The central curriculum was sacrifice, and the commencement exercise was entry into the Kingdom of God which was at hand.

I doubt that the public schools of today can be expected by you and me to touch the hem of the garment of the Master Teacher's seamless robe. But I am confident that we have many committed and competent public school teachers who by living example lead transforming lives that inspire children, as I was inspired, to consecrate their intelligence to sacred callings in every walk of life. They are burdened down by bureaucratic red tape in administratively top-heavy school systems. I do not recall "school prayers" of any kind in my public school days. I do recall the Christian concern of my teachers for me as a person. I know teachers in the public schools who live their prayers out in the lives of their students. They do so by *believing* in them when they don't believe in themselves. They do so by challenging the best in their students more than they scold the worst in them. To them their students are neither male nor female, black nor white, brown nor yellow, rich nor poor. They are persons made in the image of God and for whom Christ died. Few can be taught this way and not feel the difference and give thanks for it. They become disciples of such teachers and respond to them as Thomas Wolfe did to Margaret Roberts.

The answer to factory education is more of this kind of teacher and fewer hassles within school boards, fewer political hacks who make the schools their platform as they take firm grips on half-truths, and more parental comradeship with them in the nurture of children and youth. Such teachers have my vote, my prayers, and my gratitude.

6
To Be Free
of Helplessness

In 1969 Rollo May, commenting on the emptiness and vacuity of the lives of many of his patients, said that these things were symptomatic of a deeper problem. He said that these feelings generally come from "people's feeling that they are powerless to do anything effective about their lives or the world they live in." I call this feeling *helplessness*. At several major crises in my life the struggle for freedom from helplessness has been the stuff of my struggle to be free.

Those who work with seriously ill people every day find them falling into two groupings: persons who have, as Engels described it, "given up and given in" to their situation, and persons who are actively concerned about doing something about their situation in collaboration with us. Those in the first group drift and surrender helplessly, and those in the second struggle against the tide of helplessness that threatens to engulf them. They join with us in what is often called "the therapeutic alliance."

To me, helplessness is not necessarily a sign of weakness. It can be a means of resistance, a way of maintaining one's integrity, a nonviolent form of aggression. I have encountered helplessness myself in several crucial human situations in my adult life. I will discuss three of them.

Just as I was beginning my teaching career in 1946, I had an ordinary appendectomy. Because of a wrongly administered spinal anesthesia, I sustained an injury in my lower back that

113

has several times rendered me helpless in the face of massive pain.

At several very significant points in my life, I became "unplugged" from the political power system of which I was a part and went into a state of helplessness. The most significant point came during the Vietnam War. Our son spent a total of twenty-one months during two tours of duty with the United States Navy in the Naval Inshore Riverine Assault Group. I was overpowered by my inability to do anything about the situation, the endlessness of the war, the unjustness of the Selective Service system, and the prodigal waste of human life it entailed.

A third situation of helplessness has been for me a *threatened* helplessness more than it has been a reality in itself. That is the threat of mandatory retirement. For a person who has been addicted to work as I have, this "cold turkey" treatment at the hands of institutions is terrifying to me. The word "retirement" when applied to me trips alarms and rage in my being.

My typical response to helplessness has been *rage*. Thus you might say that this chapter is a commentary on the rage of the helpless at these unique junctures of life. I want to discuss each of these crucial situations with you as they have affected my life.

Pain and Helplessness

Pain makes you think. Thought makes you wise. Wisdom makes pain bearable. So goes the Okinawan proverb. When I speak of pain here, I am not referring to psychic pain, such as grief or anxiety over an unknown, or even to the threatening outcome of a situation in life. I am speaking of physical pain, discomfort, distress, or agony that results from the stimulation or irritation of specialized nerve endings and tracts in the body. This is what happened to me when a spinal anesthesia needle damaged a disk in my lower back in 1946.

I do not want this account to be a long detailing of "my operations." Therefore I will try to make it brief. Conservative methods of diathermy and wearing a brace were used at first.

No one taught me what *I* could do about the pain; they concentrated on what *they* could do. In 1947 I underwent a neurosurgical operation for a herniated disk. This did not relieve but exacerbated the pain, which I was told I would have "to learn to live with." In addition to radicular or nerve root damage, now I had muscle spasm. No instructions were given about *how* to live with it. By 1953, the pain was interfering with sleep, work, and riding distances in a car. I went to a second neurosurgeon, who explained that only part of the disk had previously been removed. Scar tissue had complicated the site and the fifth lumbar nerve was giving me pain in the lower back and in the left leg. A second operation was performed, and I was dismissed with the instruction that if I had more pain I was to take two aspirin!

I experienced some relief that sustained me for about two years. Then the pain began to escalate again. I went to an orthopedist after this, with a burning, unremitting pain in my back and a deep rage toward neurosurgeons. The orthopedist injected me with Xylocaine but did not tell me anything other than that my back was "a mess."

My esteemed mentor Spafford Ackerly, who suffered constant pain from an osteomyelitic knee caused by a war wound in World War I, detected my back pain in January 1965, while I was a guest lecturer for him with a medical school class. He asked me to come to his office and tell him my story. This was the first physician I had talked with who used neither needles nor knives but wisdom.

He listened pensively and said: "You are bearing unnecessary pain like a hair shirt." (I had never missed a day's work because of my back.) He said: "Your surgeons have you confused." He asked to confer with my personal family physician, Walter S. Coe, M.D. They together arranged for me to go to the Mayo Clinic in 1965. I was diagnosed as having two vertebrae ankylosed, or grown together, trapping the fifth lumbar nerve. They recommended that a *third* surgery be done to separate the vertebrae, that a bone graft or fusion be built to keep them apart, and that the nerve be cleaned of scar tissue formation and rehabilitated insofar as possible.

This was done, but more than this also. They taught me that I must exercise, rest, eat properly, keep my weight down, and reshape my work and stress system. I was dramatically relieved and maintained my sense of freedom from pain until 1971—six years. I noticed that when I was desperately fatigued, the pain literally "turned on" as if someone had pushed a switch. I lived with this by resting, keeping my weight down, and using muscle relaxants on occasion but not regularly.

Then in 1971 I developed a deteriorated disk in my cervical region, affecting my left arm and hand and causing both pain and numbness in my fingers. I returned to the Mayo Clinic. I was told I needed surgery on my upper spine! I told the surgeons with much anger that I had more pain in my lower back than I had in my upper back and they had been in that one site *three* times. I told them that they were unimaginative and that I wanted them to think of some way of controlling pain besides surgery. They said: "We are not trying to *sell* you on surgery." I said: "You are actually doing so without effort, then!" They said there were conservative measures for controlling the pain and referred me to "physical medicine and rehabilitation."

There the doctors, known as physiatrists, confirmed that arthritic buildup and disk deterioration had taken place. They advised the use of traction, prescribed exercise, and heat. These were things *I* could do, but, they said, most patients simply expected doctors to fix their pain or give them medicines to make them unaware of it. One thing they missed: the importance of rest. However, I took their program home with me and applied it with a vengeance. It worked! I kept the disciplines and outdisciplined the need for surgery. I still carried a low level of pain all the time but "put up with it" in stoical fashion. These conditions maintained until 1977, when the pain escalated.

I then went to see Barry Smith, M.D., a physiatrist at the

Institute of Physical Medicine and Rehabilitation here in Louisville. He said: "You are at about 8 out of a possible scale of 10 in pain. I could tell you to go home and stay in bed for two weeks, but your work won't let that really happen. I would like to put you in the hospital for ten days. We will lower that pain through rest and medication. Then we will teach you to handle it yourself if you will follow our instructions." This he did.

I learned that the pain was primarily due to muscle spasm, fatigue, and overweight. He taught me an elaborate set of exercises to perform morning and night. We brought the weight down to 190 pounds from 212. Results began to be dramatic. In the course of the next two years we identified another deteriorated disk in the upper back. Then we sought consultation with Roy Meckler, M.D., a neurologist, who also advised the use of daily traction. These things I did religiously and got moderately good results.

The person who taught me another key to managing the pain was Clifford Kuhn, M.D., who visited me while I was an inpatient at the rehabilitation center. He is a psychiatrist who specializes in stress-related disorders of a psychophysiologic nature. He took time out of his early morning schedule for eight interviews with me to teach me inner visualization relaxation of my whole body as an antidote to pain.

The astonishing shift in this whole process occurred when I found physicians who *teach* their patients how to take care of themselves. That was not enough. I had to give up my helplessness. I became a part of my own therapy. We formed a therapeutic alliance based upon mutual trust and shared responsibility. I later found this validated by Norman Cousins in his book *The Anatomy of an Illness*, concerning his recovery from a serious collagen disease, more specifically an ankylosing spondylitis, which means that the connective tissue of the spine was disintegrating. He said that the doctor "was wise enough to know that the art of healing is still a frontier profession," and added: "I have a hunch he believed my own total involvement was a major factor in my recovery" (p. 44).

That was the key—"my own total involvement"! I found that bondage to my own helplessness put an intolerable strain on what rudimentary knowledge my physicians had. *I expected them to fix me,* as a passive machine, not treat me as a free and living person. I was on my way to creative freedom from crippling pain when I began to be involved in the treatment myself.

Then I began to discover things about my own pain that *no* doctor had taught me. I made a decision that *fatigue* is the generator of muscle spasm, pain, and confused states of consciousness. Fatigue is directly related to overweight in that one substitutes food for rest, "quick energy," that is. I deliberately changed my sleeping and eating habits. For forty years I had firmly believed I needed no more than six or, at the most, seven hours of sleep out of twenty-four. I shifted to getting nine or ten hours sleep out of twenty-four. I copied the Mediterranean cultural habit of the siesta, or, as the French say, *faire la sieste*—"to take one's nap." I arise at 6:00 A.M. and go through my exercises and traction while listening to the morning news. I eat a light breakfast and am at my office at 7:30 A.M. I work intensively with patients, residents, and staff until 2:00 P.M. I go home and eat a light lunch and by 2:30 P.M. am in bed. I read the newspaper for fifteen minutes and then go to sleep very soon. I sleep an hour and a half, awaken, and practice inner visualization, meditation, and deep breathing for about a half hour. I then arise, answer my telephone calls, and write until the dinner hour around 7:00 P.M. My wife and I converse and read, watch television, or visit friends for two or three hours. I am in bed by 10:00 P.M.

I can go for weeks with minimal pain with this routine. When I make travel and speaking plans, I observe as much of these disciplines as I can. If I have emergencies that call for a "forced march" that breaks this routine, I know that I am setting the pain process in motion. Only I, with the tutelage and power of the Holy Spirit, can stop it. No longer do I feel the helpless rage toward doctors, especially neurosurgeons, that I did. Being free of the helplessness frees me of the rage. The rage itself was *one* source—not the only one—of pain.

I am sure I will have major battles with pain from now on. There is no such thing as *eternal* vigilance, which is proverbially said to be the price of liberty. If there were, I should think it would be quite destructive. That much vigilance lasts beyond death. However, there is such a thing as *personally responsible* vigilance. That is the price of liberty from chronic pain and the rage that it generates toward your world. Pain makes you think; thought makes you wise; wisdom makes your pain both less and bearable.

Helplessness in the Face of the Political Disfranchisement of the Vietnam War

The very word "franchise" means freedom from servitude or restraint. To have freedom from servitude or restraint, in either the political or the theological sense, is to have received it at the hands of people who are given to liberality, generosity, and magnanimity. It is, before God, to have received grace and to be loosed from the deadening power of the law.

To be disfranchised is to suffer loss of freedom from servitude at the hands of persons to whom freedom, gratitude, and grace are strangers, people who are intoxicated with the need for power. To be disfranchised is to be filled with rage—whether expressed passively or aggressively—toward those who have dispossessed us and toward our own helplessness. If you and I are in real danger from those who have dispossessed us, from the right to make our own decisions, then you and I alternate between rage and despair. Protection from either of the painful states is apathy. The end result is helplessness.

Let me describe one or two situations in my life that let you know that I have "been there."

In the time span of 1968 through 1969, I experienced a serious disfranchisement of my life in relation to the Vietnam War. I had voted for Lyndon Johnson rather than Barry

Goldwater for one reason. He promised us that he would never use American troops in Vietnam. Later I learned that he had advance intelligence during the campaign that slated an entry of our ground troops into combat with the North Vietnamese-Vietcong forces. By September of 1968, my own son was a machine gunner in the Riverine Assault Group of Naval Inshore Operations. He was and is a patriotic person who chose to fight for his country. Yet I felt that the war was there to claim his loyalty. The war itself was a severe miscarriage of justice. The President of the United States had broken faith with the nation by involving a small part of the nation's youth in an undeclared war. As a voting American I felt disfranchised. After his twenty-one months in combat service, my son said: "Who asked me? What voice did I have? None!" He went through the surrealistic Apocalypse II and returned with two Purple Hearts but in excellent health, thanks to outstanding medical care.

Yet the cumulative weight of my own anxiety about his well-being and safety was at heart an ever-increasing sense of helplessness from having been disfranchised from the whole process. My colleague Henlee Barnette had a son in the Air Force in Vietnam and at the same time had another son who refused to be drafted and fled to Sweden. Barnette and I swam through a sea of helpless rage over this situation.

In my despair, I conversed with my physician colleagues, particularly Walter S. Coe, M.D., who gave me an appointment at the end of the day so we could talk. My good friend Leslie Van Nostrand, M.D., of whom I have spoken before, called me and told me he had sensed that I was fighting a single-handed battle and wanted to pay me a visit at my home. He pointed out how both my son and my job had been such *ideals* for me that they had become *idols* for me. My life was meant for more than this. Whereas some people were uncommitted or undercommitted to their family and job, I was overcommitted to the point of absurdity. He could not have been more accurate with anyone than he was with me.

As I look back on this disfranchisement of the Vietnam War, I

can see that painful though it was, I was being delivered up out
of an idolatry of institutions—the Federal Government and all
the others. These had become "flat earths" for me, worlds unto
themselves, and my world was constricted by them. Even my
love for my son, who was unto me as Absalom was to David, had
become the central, controlling motif of my life. To let this
happen was to do violence to him, because any son can receive
the love of his father and thrive; but no son can be *the* object of
worship of his father and continue to thrive and do well. From
this too I was being delivered, and he was being disburdened!
The first lines of the Presbyterian catechism took on a new
meaning for me: "Man's chief end is to glorify God and to enjoy
him forever." In leaving my family of origin to pursue the work
of ministry in the years prior to the birth of our children, I had
embraced fully the words of Jesus in Mark 10:29-30, in the
following form: "Truly, I say to you, there is no one who has left
house or brother or sisters or mother or father . . . or lands, for
my sake and for the gospel, who will not receive a hundredfold
now in this time, houses and brothers and sisters and mothers
. . . and lands, . . . and in the age to come eternal life."

Now, however, I read it in a whole new light. Notice that the
above paragraph selectively deletes "children" twice and "with
persecutions" once. That is what the falsely self-styled
inerrantists miss about the Scriptures. With the most fervent
perfectionism about the Bible, their mind, my mind, anybody's
mind tends to *delete* that which demands the most humanity,
character, and consecration of us. My mind had deleted the
part about children meaning too much to us and the part about
having people intentionally disfranchise us, i.e., from our point
of view, persecute us! So there, just like everyone else, I
wanted to be an exception where the going got rough.

Forced Retirement and Helplessness

A third example of the dilemma of helplessness that I have
managed to avoid thus far is forced retirement. I am in my

sixty-fifth year, but I have had skirmishes and battles with the *threat* of forced retirement. If you are a younger reader, my story may give you a pattern of action for long-term planning for your later years. If you are in your fifties or sixties, this may be a sharing with a fellow struggler. If you are past sixty-five or seventy, you may be able to share secrets of dealing with the realities of forced retirement.

The first intimations of the threat of retirement grabbed me when a colleague of mine, eleven years older, was forced, much against his will, to retire. He did not really know what his work status was until six months before he had to retire. Nor could he get a straight story as to his status. The days passed, the weeks passed. He began to feel increasingly helpless because his pension funds had been poorly handled by his employer. Finally, he asked his immediate supervisor what his status was. He was told that his contract could not be renewed because the decision makers questioned his loyalty to the institution.

Immediately I urged my friend to join me in the search for another job. Providentially, former colleagues of ours saw to it that he was happily employed elsewhere. That was in 1972. Today, ten years later, he is still working quite productively on that job, though he is "retired" from the previous one.

I tell you this story in order to say that at that time I was fifty-five years of age. The gut-level question was thrust at me as to my stance toward being caught in that state of helplessness, powerlessness, and even the feeling of uselessness that he endured for a span of six months. God had delivered him. What could I learn from his painful experience?

As if this were not enough, I began to get letters and long-distance telephone calls from widely diverse areas of the country in which people told me that they had heard that I was retiring. The rumor persisted. I think it may have been at least partly due to the close association friends of ours knew existed between me and the colleague of whom I have just spoken. Yet the long series of such messages still remains a mystery to me.

The creative value of the strange confluence of events was to force me to face the issue of forced retirement *ten years* before I was to be faced with mandatory retirement at sixty-five. I began to search the literature on retirement. I conferred with my physician about my health. I surveyed the options for other employment for myself. I sought foundation grants to support my tenure as a professor at the Southern Baptist Seminary, to no avail. Nevertheless, I decided to create an open-ended kind of work situation that would permit me to work after the age of sixty-five. I resolved that pension funds, Social Security, and savings were "disability insurance" to me, not retirement money. I decided that *for me* retirement, as such, was not a necessity and not an option to be considered. I would work as long as God gave me good health. I committed myself to use the intelligence he had given me to pursue a way of life that would contribute to health and not disease.

I have told you, in the chapter on "factory education," some of the most important events that led to my resignation at the Southern Baptist Theological Seminary in 1973, ending my tenure there in 1974. One of the more profound reasons for that change of work was that I too would be terminated at the age of sixty-five regardless of the significance for my well-being. It was a rule handled legally and not personally. I would be no exception. There was no use debating, discussing, or fretting in helplessness over it. That would be wasted breath, sleep, and peace of mind, all of which are precious necessities for a healthy life and an unhindered witness for Jesus Christ.

I went to the University of Louisville School of Medicine on a "three-fourths" contract, quite the same as physicians in academic medicine. This contract requires three-fourths teaching time of me. The other fourth of the time I have complete freedom on a schedule that I arrange to lecture in other parts of the country, to do research, to write, and to do personal counseling on a fee-taking basis. The income that comes from these is my own, although I return the counseling fees to the budget of the program in ethics and pastoral counseling which I direct. It has been my purpose to develop this "one-fourth" of my work into a self-employment structure. I have been effective in accomplishing this goal. My work as a lecturer, an author, an editor, a consultant, and a pastoral counselor has enriched the teaching I do with theological students, pastors, medical students, and psychiatric residents. The internal consistency of the diversified efforts presents a minimum of frustration and a maximum of satisfaction and creativity. The opportunity to make new friends and expand the horizons of my understanding has been awe-inspiring to me.

Until the spring of 1981, I fully expected to retire from the University of Louisville. The difference would be that I had developed my self-employment capability to the point that it could—and still can—be turned rather quickly into a full-time earning capacity. I did not feel trapped, helpless, and at the mercy of circumstances beyond my control. The struggle to be free from these feelings was being rewarded by the Providence of God and the renewal, fresh strength, and intensified sense of purpose and calling God gave me. My health improved dramatically and the level of physical pain decreased and became more manageable. The freedom to plan my own schedule was a real liberation. A minimum of administrative meetings and a maximum of student and patient contact was invigorating.

Not the least of the renewal I experienced has been the opportunity to reestablish old friendships as well as form new ones. I have found that this is one of the secrets of grace for the person in later maturity: the recementing of relationships formed in the past. Doing this taps sources of power for the renewal of my life and also for influence to commend, introduce, and encourage younger men and women who are "getting their start" in the ministry, in medicine, and in the other professions as I have opportunity.

These have all been fruits of the struggle to be free from the threat of forced retirement. As if this were not enough, the chairman of the department and the dean of the School of Medicine and the president of the University in 1981 recommended to the trustees of the University to extend my tenure from 1982 to 1987. Thus the end of my contract with the University extends until I shall have become seventy years of age, the Lord willing. I said to our chairman, Dr. John Schwab: "You have not only given me life and freedom to work, but you have now given me more of it." The astounding thing about this set of events is that I did not ask for it to happen, nor did I know that it was in the making. I was surprised by joy and generosity!

The reality of retirement happens to people all around me. One friend becomes ill at sixty-one and struggles with what he calls "burnout" on his job. In his helplessness he considers "early retirement." He has no avocation, no all-consuming hobby, and his retirement benefit shrinks in its worth before his eyes. I struggle and contend with him that his life is not "over." Another friend is a part of a "reduction in force" of the company with which he has worked for thirty years. He is fifty-nine. He demands full disability pay and gets it. Now—what is he going to do with the rest of his life? Stay angry? Get fat? Stay drunk? Just work at amusing himself? Or does he have skills that can put him to work at a self-employed task that earns money, enriches his life with new purpose, and extends the days of his years?

Masses of people are in fretful helplessness now because of the "insecurity" of the Social Security system. Others who are still working see their contributions to Social Security decrease their monthly earnings more and more while the nightly news leaves them feeling that this is a shaky investment. Yet neither group can *do* anything specific about it beyond writing letters to Congress, lobbying, and voting. Even so, all of us are comparatively helpless in dealing with this system. We can be genuinely grateful that these benefits make a real difference in millions of people's lives. Yet at the same time we ask to be spared the fate of having this as the one alternative for life's basic needs of food, clothing, and shelter. Specters of the Great Depression haunt people in their late fifties, in their sixties and their seventies. Before God, what can we make of all this endemic helplessness?

The Need to Be "Taken Care of" and the Power of God: An Invitation to Dialogue

Whatever your age or sex, whatever your marital, parental, educational, or economic status, let me ask you about helplessness in your own life. To what extent is it springing from an underlying assumption of yours and mine that we are supposed to be taken care of by somebody else? Dowling called this the "Cinderella Complex" in women, the blind and naive assumption that *somebody else will take care of you,* no matter what else happens. I am persuaded that *men* also assume this. We just expect a different set of *somebodies* to take care of us. A woman may or may not expect a man to take care of her. The man, however, *may* expect the woman to take care of him, no matter whether he works or not. The man who works, as is true of many women who work, expects the company, the labor union, the Federal Government, the Social Security system, the college or university, the seminary, or a denomination or local church to take care of him or her, no matter what.

The key phrase in the above paragraph is "no matter what." You and I put that "other" who is to take care of us "no matter what" in full charge of our lives when we do this. We put all power in the other's hands. Our destiny as persons stands or falls with his or her destiny. Is this not putting into fallible, changing, fickle, and sometimes deceptive people and institutions a kind of faith that rightly belongs to God? The arm of flesh *will* fail you, the hymn says. The hymn is right. As my colleague Henlee Barnette says: "Love all persons fully; trust only God fully."

Turning over our lives to be "taken care of" is a unique loss of freedom and a bondage in its own right. When you and I do this, we are putting that which is relative in the place of the absolute.

Paul Tillich called this the source of the demonic in human life. We are totally possessed by a finite idol that becomes demonic for us. The person, institution, or job constricts our lives and we "orbit" around this center which we have exalted to a position that militates against the power of God. The struggle to be free of these kinds of possession is a lifelong one. The tempter in these matters only departs from us for a season and waits for "an opportune time" (Luke 4:13).

We are called not unto the kind of helplessness that puts us at the mercy of such demonic possession. We are called—you and I—to look only to God to be cared for "no matter what." It is heartening to have many friends who are steadfast "through thick and thin." But our relationship to them and their patience with us wear thin when we expect everything and any need to be supplied by them. Even in marriage we jeopardize the marriage itself when we expect our spouse to supply *all* our needs, no matter what. There is a vast difference between *loving* one's spouse and worshiping that person.

To the contrary, as Paul says in II Cor. 10:3-5: "Though we live in the world we are not carrying on a worldly war. . . . We destroy arguments and every proud obstacle to the knowledge of God, and take every thought captive to obey Christ." Such a worship of Christ puts all other sources of care in their places. They are channels of God's grace to us as we cast all our anxieties upon God, for he cares for us (I Peter 5:7). Through pain, through wars, through the threats of unemployment, retirement, and disability I can say that renewal comes through the unasked-for grace of God as he gives me a sense of strength and courage and channels his grace through people from whom I would have least expected it.

You may be justified in saying: "All that is too general for me. Can you make it more specific?" The answer is yes. The main reason we get trapped in the helplessness state is that we let ourselves become fixed and set into one role, function, work, or relationship and expect that never to become obsolete. There was a time when being a father or mother, a farmer, a blacksmith, a General Electric or General Motors assembly worker, a teacher in one school, or a minister in one church, or engaging in any other profession or calling was a *lifetime* thing. Now things change *too fast*. We are caught again and again in future shock, and if we insist on staying in the enclaves of the past, they will all the more quickly immobilize us into states of helplessness. We begin to think that life is over.

Yet if we are of the faith that adventures, and of the mind that continues to learn, we are no longer guided by the fixed rules of fixed roles and functions. These either do not become our gods or cease to be our gods. We are guided in faith by the living God instead, the God who moves us but moves with us, the God who leads us by a cloud by day and a pillar of fire by night. From him comes our strength and courage for the living of these days. From him comes the renewal of our lives.

7

To Be Free
from the Slavery of Overcommitment

At several points in the previous chapters of this book, I have referred obliquely or directly to the issue of commitment. The issue in the struggle to be free from poverty is partly that of the commitment to do so, the motivation to "get out of here." Obeying the command of God to "go from your country and your kindred and your father's house," as Abraham was told to do (Gen. 12:1), is no easy thing. It takes a remarkable thrust of internal initiative and external social pressure to break out of the poverty system.

In the struggle to be free of feelings of inferiority, Alfred Adler has made it clear that such feelings can take one in the opposite direction and produce an overreaction of arrogance, multiplied effort, and compensation. As negative as these are, they elicit a kind of determined pride that is a seedbed for overcommitment.

My struggle to be free of pack thinking seems to be a commitment to independence that is little short of being fierce. I find the pressure to conform even among the noisiest nonconformists, and it has to be resisted.

My struggle to be free of loneliness, furthermore, implicitly demanded that I have both the capacity and the intention to commit myself to love others as much as myself or, as Harry Stack Sullivan compassionately says, "almost as oneself." The intensity of a two-way relationship of intimacy that has offset loneliness in my life has produced an intensity of commitment that has not always been according to wisdom.

Again, my resistance to mass education in this country with its top-heavy administration and bureaucratic manipulation of huge populations in crowded cities has made commitments to a personalized educational process a form of hazardous duty that calls for a kind of eccentric overcommitment. Trying too hard has become a way of life to be chastened by age, experience, and better judgment.

Finally, my struggle to be free of helplessness has elicited a resolve in my consciousness in the face of pain or disfranchisement that has made wholehearted participation in the relief of my situation imperative. Where commitment to the process of deliverance from my bonds of helplessness ends and where loss of spontaneity begins is hard to determine. Overcommitment in all these instances can become a way of life. The story of my life has been overcommitment.

For me and probably for you and many others, *overcommitment* can become a bondage of the human will, a compulsion to do more and more *for* our family, our institution, our cause. Out of this come the negative side effects of our struggle to be free. We have had excellent studies of uncommitment, such as that by Kenneth Keniston (*The Uncommitted: Alienated Youth in American Society*; Harcourt, Brace & World, 1965). Andras Angyal comments on several ways of finding some sort of balance in human life. He speaks of having a set of safe rules to live by; he describes desperate dogmatism that "arbitrarily overshouts doubt." Then he gives a name to the "overall method of dealing with the demands and challenges of life." He calls it "the life-style of noncommitment." Whether it is called noncommitment, being "laid back," or whatever, this life-style has not been mine. Yet I cannot condemn people so inclined. Their compulsions work in a reverse gear, mine is a forward gear. Both are bondages in their own right.

The problem of uncommitment, being "laid back," has never been my Achilles' heel. Mine has been *over*commitment. This is a subject about which highly specialized studies have, at least to my knowledge, not been done. Most of what I know about overcommitment I have found out the hard way—by being overcommitted and feeling the counterproductive clutches of this life-style in the pain pathways of my body, by sensing the results in strained relationships to uncommitted or partially committed co-workers, and by getting wisdom about it from people who were committed, but who were so "according to knowledge" and who were believers in moderation in all things.

When I talk about overcommitment, I must first enter a disclaimer. Our Lord, when dying on the cross, said in words from Ps. 31:5, "Father, into thy hands I commit my spirit!" just before he breathed his last (Luke 23:46). God redeemed him from death through the power of the resurrection. Someone may say: "We must be *that* committed. Is that what *you* mean by overcommitment?"

My response is that Jesus intended that we should take up our crosses daily, die to overcommitment to all earthly idols, and experience the freedom of walking in the newness or renewal of life in him. Obedience to the Lordship of the risen Christ is the most effective antidote for our idolatry of causes, goals, institutions, ministerial roles, physicians' roles, or even to our spouses or grown sons and daughters. That obedience to him provides a simplicity, integrity, and freedom from undue anxiety. We try to *be* Jesus! He has already done a perfect job of that. In short, the overcommitted are prone to be self-appointed saviors.

I recall becoming quite ill in my first pastorate. I went to a rural physician who said that I was suffering indigestion from eating too much greasy food. He advised me to avoid fried foods. Then he said: "There's something else wrong too." Puzzled, I asked what. He replied: "You are a young pastor. You are trying too hard. You are trying to be Jesus. It won't work. He's already gotten there first. You are just one of his men putting in a good word for him. Keep doing that, but don't try to replace him. It can't be done." He had given me more wisdom than I knew at the time. He had put his finger on my spiritual Achilles' heel.

The Tempering of Overcommitment

To bring some balance, order, and design into my life of overcommitment I have, since 1968, undergone an agonizing reappraisal of my way of life. I have struggled to identify and temper its sources in my life. I have done so in several ways.

First, I have observed myself and other people and am convinced that *genetics of an unspecified and variant kind* provides the mood-swinging temperament out of which overcommitment is made. Such a temperament is characterized by periods of one's life when one is bursting with energy, sees little need for rest, and vigorously accomplishes several difficult tasks all at once. When success attends these overproductive periods, as has been true for me, I have become energized all the more. Many successful persons continue on this kind of momentum for years at a time. Sometimes it is popularly called living on nervous energy.

However, I have seen exhaustion set in and I will lose momentum. I may become irritable, fall into conflict with those around me, and become generally unhappy. I am fortunate to have a wise wife and group of colleagues at work who have joined humorously and lovingly in slowing me down, demanding that I rest, and applauding me for paying attention to them. My genetic makeup is the gift of what is called a Type A personality. Hans Selye speaks of "stress-seeking persons." My own life history causes me to feel that biogenetically I was put together this way. As Ps. 139:13 puts it, "Thou didst form my inward parts, thou didst knit me together in my mother's womb." I have known and accepted this about myself since early adolescence as God's unique gift to me to be guided and utilized by the intelligence he also gave me. I have never seen it as a curse to be bemoaned, but as a vast reservoir of renewable energy to be used, not burnt out, in fulfilling my destiny.

I have also concluded that the driving force of my overcommitment has been to be accepted, to prove myself worthy, to be a welcome part of the community of those whose approval I consider most worthwhile. Early in my life, I felt like an outsider in my family. As I grew to be six inches taller than any other member of my family, I learned to use my body aggressively and was no longer someone to be pushed around. The pages in Washington and my brothers at home learned this. But this—with my intense interest in education—once again made me the "outlandish" one. Yet I needed affirmation and overcompensated to get it.

As I entered college, academic achievement was my basis for acceptance by professors, but a basis for discomfort and rejection by many peers. Nobody loves a smart aleck. Yet I was overcommitted to academic excellence. As I entered the seminary I found my acceptance in a few intimate fellow students and a significant number of the faculty. Nevertheless, I chose a field of study that was lowly regarded and grudgingly approved. Massive overcommitment was required to hew out a place in the curriculum for it.

For twenty-seven years, night and day, I directed my energy to receiving the approval of my peers for the place and legitimacy of, and the professional necessity for, equipping a minister with wisdom and skill in pastoral care and the psychological and psychiatric sciences. It was a grueling effort at excellence based on the dogged assumption that excellence would bring approval, acceptance, and a genuine sense of belonging. I had little or no time for camaraderie, shared golf games, denominational political discussions, or even much of the amenities of entertaining or being entertained on social occasions in the home.

Remarkably enough, as I describe this now, I see that a large majority of my colleagues—though not all—were similarly overcommitted, similarly eager for approval, similarly asocial, lonely, and isolated. They simply did different things from what I did. The absence of a sense of community among us, it seems to me, had been the social result of large numbers of over-committed people working not together but in the same geographical location. We were doubly overcommitted—to the institution itself, as a world unto itself, and to our own particular kinds of expertise, each of which had a language system of its own.

This leads to a third source of the driving force of overcommitment in my life—professional specialization. The average lay person has not the slightest idea of how overspecialized a relatively large theological faculty can be. The person in one office or classroom is using a nomenclature untranslatable by the professor in the next classroom. Whole different language systems arise and develop a life of their own. Those who speak a given language speak best to each other; at times they speak *only* to each other. Consequently, our primary loyalty group becomes professors in distant schools who also understand our nomenclature. This happened to me.

The end result of this is a whole faculty of people starved for approval and acceptance by each other. In the intense hunger for this we redouble our efforts, we become all the more productive and specialized in what we are doing, overcommitted afresh with the hope that we will be recognized, accepted, respected, and applauded as professionals in our fields of specialty. It is a lonely crowd!

A fourth and powerful dynamic in my overcommitment has been the vow I made as I struggled free from poverty. The vow is that, God being my helper, I shall never be poor again. A person who has made such a vow is always piling up a surplus. It is not enough to have a medical insurance plan; one must have a "backup" or contingency plan as well. This vow is fueled by fear. I have always looked over my shoulder to see if poverty was gaining on me. Being competent at earning a living at *one* thing has not been enough; I have developed two or three and sometimes four competencies that are income-producing. If I can attach a two-week vacation to one speaking engagement that involves travel, I can pay our way out of current earnings. I

can get along without a suit until it has been marked down and is
on sale. I rarely have borrowed money unless I already had the
money invested at a higher rate of interest to pay it back. Even a
house mortgage to me was a threat; I struggled to pay off a
thirty-year mortgage in twelve years and succeeded. This kind
of overcommitment to having a backup surplus, to staying out of
debt, and to having more than one way of making a living has
produced a kind of overcommitment to work. I have written
about this in my book *Confessions of a Workaholic* (1971). I
sought to affirm the laboring person's right to rest in a
tongue-in-cheek book entitled *Workaholics: Make Laziness
Work for You* (1978). (Both of these books are now in paperback
editions with Abingdon Press.) Later I expressed my more
serious and positive experience in resolving the overcommitment at work in my book *Nurturing Silence in a Noisy Heart*
(Doubleday & Co., 1979).

A fifth factor related to my overcommitment is *being
underpaid*. For all of the years I was employed in the
institutions of the church, I was tacitly expected and
economically driven to put in overcommitted hours of work in
order to pay the bills for my family and myself. Many
engagements would have been refused except for the harsh
necessity of paying bills that remained despite a severely
disciplined and austere life-style. I learned early in my career
that the teaching profession, even within churches that value
education all out of proportion to its real functional value, is
ubiquitously underpaid.

This same thing can be said of pastors of churches as well. I
recall conferring in a retreat with a group of Lutheran pastors
and their wives. Late in the conference, the economic anxiety
of the group surfaced. They spoke of the rigors they were
undergoing in order to pay their bills. I suggested that a
professionally compatible kind of work be learned by the
pastors. For example, a rural pastor could work as a substitute
teacher in the public schools to supplement his or her income.
Then they told me that the rules of the presiding officers of their

section of the Lutheran Church did not permit this. I said: "The apostle Paul made tents!" Then the wife of one of the pastors quickly responded: "The pastor's *wife* is the tentmaker with a second income!"

The study entitled *Ministry in America* (ed. by Merton P. Strommen et al.; Harper & Row, 1980) reveals that *the* most expected characteristic of ministers by their congregations and themselves is "service without regard to acclaim" (p. 17). The formal agenda here is that the minister does his or her work with a spirit of abandon, and without an eye to public recognition. The hidden assumption, however, is that the minister will not (and will not expect to) be appropriately paid for his or her work. After forty years of being a minister and working with ministers, I can say that I have seen ministers who are greedy for money and conspicuous symbols of affluence. But for each one of these I have seen, there are probably five hundred who are underpaid and never complain. Furthermore, the inability to say "no" to too much work and the ability to pay one's bills are directly related.

Overcommitment for me, further, has sprung from my inability to say "no" even when my livelihood is not an issue. The need for recognition, the need for an ego-retread, the need to be in the limelight, all prompted my overcommitment on every hand. However, with both economic and ego needs in mind, the way that I have found of saying "no" is to ask whether or not I can *competently* fulfill the task I am being asked for a commitment to do. When I limit my commitment to that which I am both competent to fulfill and able to find the time and energy to prepare for, then reason, good judgment, and personal serenity reflect that I do not become overcommitted.

This latter wisdom, however, has come to me since I moved into a work situation in which I am not underpaid. I do not believe that economics *determines* our destiny. I do think that economics *shapes* our thoughts and decisions far more than the pious people of the earth know or are willing to admit.

These are a few of the driving forces that have made me an

overcommitted person. My own deliverance from overcommitment is still in process. This has been, as I have said, the schema, the pattern, the script of my life: "Give it more than you have to give!"

Deliverance from Overcommitment

Deliverance from overcommitment starts when, in our late thirties, we are confronted with the outcomes of our earlier decisions. Often we are married, have adolescent sons and daughters, and are well into whatever work we have chosen. We hit the snags, the frustrations, the frailties of our life situation. In the years from thirty-six to forty-two we tend to be forced to face up to our limitations and to our overextension of ourselves. Up to this point, we have known no limits. We have promised everything to everybody. Then the day of reckoning comes. We must make good those promises, fulfill those commitments, come to terms with the limits of our health and energy.

If you did or are doing what I did at this time, you probably have simply doubled your efforts. You tell yourself you are not trying hard enough and things will change if you just commit yourself all the more.

That is what I did at age forty-one, at the institution where I was then working. I simply forgot about improving my aim and accepted more and more responsibility. I accomplished a prodigious amount of work, but by the time I was forty-eight I met the great limitation of an injured and osteoarthritic spine. The pain itself called my hand a third time, asking for a change of life-style. I learned little from it and was only to be taught well by it at age sixty. You can see how slowly I learn!

A confluence of events occurred when I became a professor in the School of Medicine. The first thing was an awesome event. These persons were predominantly physicians, nurses, medical and psychiatric social workers, and psychologists. Whereas I saw myself as a "specialist in pastoral care and counseling," they saw me as an educated and certified pastor and theologian. I was expected to function as a professional in their sense of the word, i.e., that I was disciplined in a technical knowledge of the whole field of theological studies, not just one. Furthermore, when I did function with authority in these areas, they *accepted* me as a professional who really knew what I was doing. This acceptance was *new* to me. I found it hard to believe. This loosened the grip of the compulsion to overcommit myself. I did not feel the need any longer to knock myself out to get approval. I began to relax and rethink my priorities.

A second thing I learned from this medical setting is that although these persons work long hours, nevertheless they have a deep respect for each other's time off duty. In part, they have an off-duty and on-duty system made possible by "covering the service" for each other, each taking his or her turn. This is a concept unknown in the Christian ministry. Therefore, it was only a short while before they enabled me to have a colleague in Dr. Henlee Barnette and a system of residents, so that we too have someone to cover for us during our time off duty. This sets distinct limits on commitment, whereas ministers in the parish and in theological faculties have the fictitious goal of being omnipresent. This discovery further disciplined my overcommitment with good judgment.

A third thing my colleagues did to help me to bring my overcommitment into field was to demand that I take my health very seriously. This is their area of expertise. They have seen to it that the precise disciplines for controlling the spinal pain were prescribed. They monitor me regularly on a planned basis. In turn, they permit me to care for them at times of difficult professional crises, times of career decision, times of the weddings of their daughters and sons, and times of severe grief. An amazing gift of grace is mine when I see these incursions of genuine koinonia around me. The very choice of the medical profession is a commitment to considerable loneliness of decision-making. I find that I can with the simplicity of being present, being a friend, and being a good listener assuage their loneliness at the same time that they help me curb my overcommitment.

Overcommitment in an Emergency Hospital

As I have been writing this chapter, I have had the responsibility of enabling two patients to be admitted to the hospital on an emergency basis. Both of them are acutely ill, one of them is severely suicidal. The other is so bizarre in her actions that she has shaken the respect of her children. It has taken much time, energy, and patience to see to it that these patients are adequately cared for and that they and their families' needs are considered very tenderly. This has involved intense teamwork with chaplains, physicians, nurses, social workers, admitting officers—all of whom are highly trained exceptionally competent, and dedicated persons. Yet I stand back from the stress and strain of the situation and have to admit that to do this work right each of us has to be called to a service that is ordinarily "over and above the line of duty." It causes us to "stretch every nerve, and press with vigor on," as Philip Doddridge's hymn from the 1700s puts it.

Overcommitment becomes a way of life with us. Fatigue is a built-in presupposition. Long hours are the norm and not the exception. When probed, one of these professionals will shrug and say: "It comes with the territory!"

More specifically and significantly, the field of psychiatry, in the context of which I work as a theologian and pastor, has its own unique overcommitment pattern as a specialty profession within medical science. Though I am not a psychiatrist, the same concerns about patients come with my territory as I work in a department of psychiatry. These words are being written shortly after John Hinckley was declared "not guilty of shooting the President of the United States and several other persons by reason of insanity." Many psychiatrists gave testimony for and against Hinckley. The issue of *which* psychiatrist's opinion had the most weight was not raised. My own common sense tells me that the opinion of the physician who cared for him over the longest period after the event should bear the most weight because she had the best opportunity to observe him and knew him best. Yet the outcome was not tempered by these considerations. Predicting criminal behavior as legal testimony very quickly becomes an overextension of psychiatrists.

Furthermore, psychiatrists are held legally responsible for keeping people alive who have decided to kill themselves. If a patient succeeds in his or her efforts at suicide, then the physician is often held responsible for having "let," "caused," "failed to prevent," or "neglected" the patient's actions. I have had one counselee who killed himself, and I know that no *one* person can take the responsibility for another's suicide. To do so is overcommitment.

I think that this kind of societal expectation of the physician demands more of one human being than is realistic, just, or wise. I feel this keenly now because I am professionally bonded with these colleagues. For the psychiatric profession to accept this kind of responsibility is to be overcommitted beyond the range of human capability. For example, psychiatrists at St. Elizabeth's Hospital in Washington, D.C., are being *legally* expected to predict whether or not John Hinckley will try to kill again. To accept this kind of responsibility is more than simply "giving the benefit of the doubt" or "going out on a limb" for a given patient. It is a professional overcommitment, and the profession as a whole would be wise to reject this expectation.

This kind of overcommitment concerns me deeply because I myself repeatedly find myself caring for people who are either actively suicidal, homicidal, or both. Similarly, I have often been part of a team that follows up the results of both suicides and homicides. In an effort to see to it that people who are severely ill or who have chronic character disorders are treated humanely, both physicians and ministers have angled themselves into a corner of overcommitment that is beyond any human being's capacity to fulfill. Social responsibility has been tilted. Individuals can blame their acts on parents, society in general, and physicians in particular. They can adopt personal irresponsibility as a way of life. This habit is the hardest to kick of all the addictions that beset us. Some cooperative kicking of the habit of accepting too much responsibility for the behavior of others by psychiatrists would create initial withdrawal symptoms but in the long run do more people more good.

Overcommitment in the Eyes of God: An Invitation to Dialogue

When you and I turn aside and ask how God must perceive overcommitment, fresh angles of vision are a renewing grace. The need to be a god; the need to be without limits; the need to have full control; the need to be a savior; the need to exercise absolute freedom—these needs prompt overcommitment. In fact, the very title of this book, "The Struggle to Be Free," is a plump fruit of enticement to the fanfare of an *absolute* freedom. Human finitude, limitations, and fallibility being real, there is no such thing as absolute freedom. Yet the temptation to assume that there is—when yielded to, however subtly—is the heart of overcommitment. We assume that if we eat of this fruit, which is "good for food," a "delight to the eyes," and "to be desired to make one wise," we will "be like God." But to act on this assumption makes us naked before God. The need to cover ourselves with the neat rationalization of "wanting to be of help" is a knee-jerk response of ministers, physicians, nurses social workers, and psychologists.

Søren Kierkegaard described the inner tensions of human nature by saying that we are always caught in the tension between our finitude and the hunger for infinitude, between our confinement to the necessities of life and our hunger to fulfill our possibilities, and between the strictures of our consciousness and our quest to know our unconsciousness (*The Sickness Unto Death*, pp. 44-77; Princeton University Press, 1941).

To find a relative and functional freedom in life is to be committed to staying at work between these polarities but not to succumb to either. Overcommitment absorbs us in either finitude or infinitude, necessity or possibility, consciousness or unconsciousness.

Erich Fromm relates overcommitment to idolatry. He says that "the history of mankind up to the present time is primarily the history of idol worship, from the primitive idols of clay and wood to the modern idols of the state, the leader, production, and consumption—sanctified by the blessing of an idolized God" (*You Shall Be as Gods*, p. 43; Holt, Rinehart & Winston, 1966). I would add to his list the worship of a given religious denomination or a professional role in the community of persons. This is the main source of our "drivenness." The overcommitted are jarred by reality when our basic humanity, limitations, and especially helplessness inevitably come rushing in upon us.

The healing for overcommitment comes with understanding and living within our basic human limitations. Freud pointed out that many of our ills come from living beyond our emotional means. The principle of the incarnation which God demonstrated in Jesus' birth, growth, and life is the opposite of our subtle needs to play God. Freedom from the tyranny of overcommitment means, not the absence of commitment, but the refusal to absolutize any loyalty other than that which we give to God. Within this steady resolve is the freedom of a genuinely human existence of which Stephen Neill speaks: "For the individual to have significance beyond himself, it is not necessary that he should have passed through an unlimited number of human experiences. All that is required is that he should be completely himself, a real person, wholly and entirely distinct from any other, and that he should remain free in relation to the circumstances in which he is called to act" (*A Genuinely Human Existence*, p. 37; Doubleday & Co., 1959). Yet when I overcommit myself or you overcommit yourself, we cannot remain free to act appropriately to the circumstances in which we are called to act. God the Creator, whose creatures we are, has set the bounds of our habitation. Only his grace can extend them. Only our search for wisdom from God can enable us to know, accept, and feel the freedom that comes to us when we accept and learn to laugh at our grandiose assumptions that those bounds of our habitation are not there.

8
Some Prizes
of the Struggle to Be Free

THE STRUGGLE to be free is not a meaningless or ambiguous fight for the love of fighting. Yet I must confess that it was a long time before I could distinguish between the struggle for survival and the struggle to be free. I did not learn quickly to live serenely in the strength of the convictions given to me through the grace of God and nurtured in silence through the power and companionship of the Spirit of God. Now, however, out of the complexity of human life have emerged some vital convictions; and these are to me "prizes" of the struggle to be free. These prizes are available to everyone, and many gifted persons I know well seem to have them as native endowments. Yet who knows? They too may have won these gifts through severe struggles to be free persons in the power of the Spirit of God. You may find the prizes I name to be aspirations of your own for which any amount of struggle would be worth the effort. Let me enumerate some of the convictions and gifts that I treasure as prizes of my own struggle to be free.

The Prize of Covenant Living
and Responsible Freedom

The first conviction that has become a prize for me is this: To be human at its best is to make mutual covenants with other people and to keep them faithfully. A covenant is mutual. Otherwise, it is not a covenant at all. It is an effort to please, appease, obligate, or even to manipulate or be manipulated by the other person.

Earlier, I spoke of the tyranny of one-way covenants in relationship to other people. Because we are human, our freedom is a finite and necessity-bound freedom. My struggle to be free has been to push back the *unnecessary*, externally and internally imposed constrictions of my freedom—constrictions not set by God in the bounds of habitation. In relation to God and to man, to break such bonds was, is, and will be a categorical imperative for me.

The surest way to increase and exercise my freedom under God is to live by covenants, accept the disciplines of the covenants I make, and enjoy the exalting sense of freedom of having faithfully fulfilled these covenants. This is the way to live the life of ethical love. To resist the exploitation of one-way covenants is to live the life of justice. To go the second mile when others break their covenants with me is to live the life of forgiveness and mercy. To seek quickly the forgiveness of those with whom I have broken a covenant is to live the life of confession and restitution. The very nature of all these dimensions of covenant living is the freedom that comes out of deep reciprocity with God and our fellow persons.

We often quote the passage: "The truth shall make you free." We engrave it in stone on public buildings built to last a thousand years. Yet in few instances does truth make you free, except to pose new dilemmas in which you will choose or not choose to discipline yourself to freedom. The truth of nuclear fission has not made us free; we are muscle-bound by the power it has given us. We are gripped by the "blink" we wait for in the eyes of adversaries when we confront them. We haggle in the bonds of indecision because we have more power than wisdom with which to handle it. We bankrupt national treasuries to keep a power that, once released, would destroy not only others but ourselves as well. The truth in this case and in many others is merely the key to a Pandora's box of restrictions of our freedom.

The unrestricted promise that the truth will make us free suggests a one-way, undisciplined covenant. Jesus never promised such freedom. To the contrary, he posed a *two-way* covenant. Notice the whole context from which this sentence is taken in John 8:31-32: "Jesus then said to the Jews who had believed in him, 'If you continue in my word, you are truly my disciples, and you will know the truth, and the truth will make you free.'" The "if " in Jesus' words embodies a commitment, an intent, a relationship, and a discipline (inseparable from "disciple"). Freedom is the fruit of the discipleship, not simply a matter of collecting true facts about the universe. Our problem is, as Robert Frost said, that we have lived "in the fond faith [that] . . . accumulated fact will of itself take fire and light the world up" (*In the Clearing*, p. 17; Holt, Rinehart & Winston, 1962).

My personal credo is embodied in the totality of the words of Jesus: If knowledge of facts apart from this kind of relationship and discipline—which runs through the highest wisdom of other *living* religions as well—does "light the world up," it may well be a holocaust of the whole world in nuclear stupidity, not the gentle rays of the sun, and certainly not the Light of the World from the eternal God.

The Prize of Being a Citizen of the Universe

Many of the struggles to be free I have described in this story of mine are struggles with the uncertainties of the institutions of our world—schools, churches, professions, and the state. When news came of the death of Leonid Brezhnev, President of the Soviet Union, I could not but be impressed with the way we as Americans and they as Soviets live without knowing each other. Yet when death strikes, the finality of it pushes us as a nation to visit them in their grief. Such visits are as eerie in their way as the space walks of the astronauts. Death and space walks remind us, if but for a short time, that the "worlds" we hasten back to are really "flat earths" to us.

One of the great prizes of the struggle to be free, especially in the context of the redemption we have in Jesus Christ, is to be liberated from the flat earths of human relationships and to become citizens of the universe. Each institution or revolution was originally established to meet a specific set of needs. The longer it survives, the more it develops a life of its own and becomes an end in itself. The institution itself becomes a world unto itself, and its members' awareness of anything *beyond* the boundaries of the institution becomes dimmer and dimmer. In effect, it becomes a "flat earth" beyond the edges of which is an abyss. Then conflicts break out because of the insulated, unventilated environment in which people rebreathe the same air, rethink the same ideas, rehash the same conflicts, and rehearse the wrongs of others.

Before intrepid explorers challenged the idea that the world was flat, certain coins of Mediterranean countries carried a picture of the Pillars of Hercules and the inscription *Ne plus ultra*—"There is nothing beyond." After the discovery that the earth is round, and that new worlds existed, the coins read: *Plus ultra*—"There is more beyond."

In the last several years I have observed the same unventilated, flat-earth thinking I had seen earlier—and hear about now—in other denominations than my own, in other seminaries, in medical schools, in churches, in social service organizations, and in government agencies. People are a part of the "in" group or a part of the "out" group; there are those on the "enemies lists" who get nothing they want. The "fair-haired ones" get everything they want and can do no wrong. Yet the whole system is in a state of entropy because there is no reinvigoration and growth by interaction with other systems. If the system is a family shut off from the world, that family is most likely to be one in which child and spouse abuse take place or in which incest occurs. Whereas abuse becomes actual in the family, it becomes symbolic or metaphorical in schools, churches, and hospitals. Students, church members, and patients become incidental or nonessential while the intra-institutional entropy prevails. After all, students, church members, and patients are from "another world." They do not belong to the settlement. They are means, not ends in themselves.

The prize of discovering the galaxies of worlds beyond my own provincial "flat earths" is a treasure to me, also. Freedom from flat-earth thinking makes one a citizen of the universe. Without this freedom, much of what professionals are fond of calling "burnout" happens. According to *The Morrow Book of New Words* (ed. by N. H. and S. K. Mager; William Morrow & Co., 1982), burnout is "a point in time or in a missile trajectory when the combustion of fuels in the rocket engine is terminated by other than programmed cut-off " (p. 41). The "programmed cut-off " would be the original mission. "Burnout" would be the result of the power source being cut off by something other than the original plan.

If we use this as a metaphor of what happens where there is flat-earth thinking, we would say simply that the institution has lost touch with its basic mission. A church, a hospital, a school is in the world to minister and not to be ministered unto. The ones that reach out go beyond their own pillars of Hercules to interact with the rest of the world and the rest of the worlds. There are galaxies of universes beyond our own little staked-out *terra firma*. To have access to the galaxies is the intention of God in Jesus Christ.

Very early in my career, Gaines Dobbins cautioned me to have *many* relationships and not just those in the job where I happened to be. Thus I maintained a consultantship with the School of Medicine for twenty-six years while teaching in the Baptist Seminary. I was a visiting professor at Union Theological Seminary in New York for two winters and eleven summers. I was an adjunct professor at Earlham School of Religion in Richmond, Indiana, for three years. I was a summer session teacher at Vanderbilt Divinity School and a visiting

professor at Princeton Theological Seminary. Yes, there were
other worlds. I dimly knew. However, it did not hit me as
breathtaking good news until I joined forces with medical
students, theological students, psychiatric residents, and
graduate students in theology in reaching out to psychotic,
suicidal, depressed, and poverty-ridden hordes of patients in
our inner-city charity hospital. Then I realized that though I
was only a block away from the preclinical students and a few
dozen blocks away from two very fine theological schools, in fact
I was as if on another planet. I was really out of that world. But
God was very much present. Yet even where I was I had
inherently the flat-earth possibility. I am grateful that I did not
have to wait to die to be free—free at last from the company
stores, plantation offices, and flat earths of this world. In one's
disfranchisement from the world, freedom is the gift of God's
bounty. Access to the galaxies of many systems of human
kinship is a cherished prize of the struggle to be free, the
intention of God for you and me from the time we were formed
in our mother's womb.

The Prize of Freedom
in Relation to Power

Another treasure trove gained in my struggle to be free is a
recently found freedom in the use of power in relation to fellow
humans and to God. You may find yourself trapped in what
Bonaro Overstreet used to call "over-under" relationships. You
feel oppressed. You may be in what is an "out" relationship to
your particular power structure. You feel ostracized. Or you
may be on the "inside" of the power structure and feel an
uneasy sense of false security. You feel apprehensive. To be
free of oppression, ostracism, and apprehension is a prize
indeed. This freedom is to be found in two relationships to
power: power at the center of things and power from the
periphery.

Power at the Center of Things. In his *Politics* Aristotle wrote that "every community is established with a view to some good; for mankind always acts in order to obtain that which they think is good" (Book I, Ch. 1). I assume that the place where the struggle for power occurs between members of the community is at the divergence of their opinions as to what they think is good. Therein lies the risk.

Power is creative when it is seen as the acceptance, and faithful discharge, of responsibility. Power brings the obligation for decision-making in behalf of the common good. Power is transmitted in the skilled craftsman's tools that saw wood or metal; it is seen in engines that can move earth or lift a plane from the ground. Power can energize creativity and discharge responsibility to do a job. Power becomes demonic, however, when it is used to posture, pose, or set oneself apart from and over others; to embellish a public image; to form an imperial coterie of one's "palace guards."

Martin Luther applied this whole set of distinctions to the clergyperson when he said: "Every clergyman in the church . . . should first of all clearly distinguish between himself and his office." Luther's observation about clergy is similar to the comment of Harry Truman concerning the Presidency. He said that the playing of "Hail to the Chief" and the firing of a twenty-one gun salute were not for Harry Truman. They were for the Presidency. He said that the President who got the feeling they were for *him* was headed for trouble.

These reflections and interpretations give substance to my sense of freedom in the use of power, particularly by a Christian, in whatever context I work. More specifically, they apply to the use of power at the center of a church, a hospital, a school, the state.

A Chinese proverb states my point of view: "If you have to have it, you can't have it; if you don't have to have it, it is yours." "It" can be anything in the proverb, but here I refer to "having to have" an office or position of power at the center of things as if your whole life depended upon it, as if it is your manifest destiny, right, and privilege to have this position of power. Offices in churches, schools, the state are like bread, shelter, and clothing for a family. Such a necessity is one of the "givens" of life. However, to take the figure a step farther, this does not give the officeholder the right to lord it over the other members of the family. If you or I hold such offices, we have a responsibility to pull our share of the load and to stay out of a permanent adversary position with "the powers that be." The "lording it over" stance spawns adversarial personalities and locks us into a "siege mentality."

My own attitude to "power at the center" positions has been that I will do such work as a *necessity* for the common good, but as a burden and not as a personal pleasure. I like the salty comment of Harry Truman: "As always, I am just trying to do the job I am supposed to do, and a lot of times in public service, that is an unusual procedure, so it causes comment" (William Hillman, *Mr. President,* p. 217; Farrar, Straus & Young, 1952). As soon as possible, I would get myself out of office after my job had been accomplished. To seek, to run for, to maneuver to get such positions tends to reduce, if not destroy, the function the position calls for. It obligates you to timeservers who later try to "collect" their political debts.

National politics has a built-in adversarial system that is sometimes effective but ordinarily not. In a Christian institution, however, the adversarial system is wrong. To stay in such a position perpetually vitiates our own morale. Worse than that, it calls for attitudes and behaviors that are antithetical to the Christian witness. As we are increasingly persuaded to fight fire with fire in behaviors similar to those of our adversary, we become in the end *like* that which we hate. If we are to be at the center of the power system, by necessity then, I think we can best do so by seeing our position as a time-limited function (six years at the most) and not as a perpetual end in itself.

The desire to stay at the center of a power structure over a lifetime is really an outworking of our need for perpetuity, i.e., to project ourselves beyond our death, to have arms that reach back from the grave and continue to shape events. This seems to be more than a subtle preoccupation of Presidents of the United States.

Power from the Periphery. Another creative way of relating to the power structure is from the periphery. Bernard Baruch, who was noted for holding park-bench consultations with government leaders in Washington, stated it best when he said that he had only a park-bench interest in administration. Paul Tillich, in his autobiographical sketch, writes: "I thought the concept of the boundary might be a fitting symbol for the whole of my personal and intellectual development. At almost every point I have had to stand between two alternative possibilities of existence, to be completely at home in neither and to take no definitive stand against either." He speaks of being between two temperaments, between social classes, between reality and imagination, between theory and practice, between church and society, between idealism and Marxism, between a native and an alien land. And he adds: "The boundary is the best place for acquiring knowledge" (*On the Boundary: An Autobiographical Sketch*, p. 13; Charles Scribner's Sons, 1966). These are two ways of describing what I mean by the peripheral existence.

I have learned from Aldous Huxley a third interpretation of being peripherally related to power. Let me quote his words: "It is not at the center, not from within the organization, that the saint can cure our regimented insanity; it is only from without, at the periphery. If he makes himself a part of the machine, in which the collective madness is incarnated, one or the other of two things is bound to happen. Either he remains himself, in which case the machine will use him as long as it can and, when he becomes unusable, reject or destroy him. Or he will be transformed into the likeness of the mechanism with and against which he works, and in this case we shall see Holy Inquisitions and alliances with any tyrant prepared to guarantee ecclesiastical privileges" (*Ape and Essence*, pp. 6-10; Harper & Brothers, 1948).

In my present situation I live on the boundary between science and religion, the rational and the nonrational, the medical establishment and the theological establishment, the rich and the poor, the powerful and the helpless. I affect somewhat the process of theological education and that of medical education. I am vitally related to both but at the periphery of each as its boundaries come together with the boundaries of the other.

I observe closely and at first hand many conflicts of power between federal, state, county, city, and private corporate interests where large amounts of money are involved. I listen intently and with great concern to competing ideologies within medicine and within the inner workings of at least five different denominations. At times I am sought as a consultant by the military on educational, morale, and chaplaincy matters. Yet I am not responsible for the outcome of any of these matters. For example, I am influential and effective in the diagnosis, treatment, patient management, and convalescent care of many sick people. The primary responsibility for the outcome, however, is in the hands of the physician. I am glad that this is so, because I affect the process from the periphery and not from the center.

The tools of ministry of the peripheral person are friendly persuasion, "no strings attached" wisdom, and an expertise wrought out of years of experience. It could well be that the prize of living a peripheral existence comes from a long-demonstrated competence that gives integrity to seniority. It may also be that the peripherally effective person is one who has made a lifework of forming and maintaining steadfast relationships to people who have that same vocation in life. In other words, the friendly persuasiveness and influence are *not* just my prerogatives as an individual. I am only one expression of the organism, power, and weight of being of what Elton Trueblood calls "the company of the committed."

Apparently, then, the church is an organism rather than an organization of special interest groups, however worthy the interest may be. The church is a reality in which the Holy Spirit is the *center* of power. All of us are at the periphery of the sovereignty of God. His Spirit knits together the influence of many people of clean hands and pure hearts, whose souls have not been lifted up to vanity, and who have not sworn deceitfully. Good judgment, justice, and the loving-kindness of God break through.

In this sense, all of us in the family and the church can share the prize of being persons of peripheral influence. We can be spoken of in the marketplace as people who do not have any ax to grind, as "free spirits," as persons with no vested interest. As we are more formally involved somewhat away from the periphery, we may be called "consultants," although that word has of late become more and more confusing and trite. In the life of local churches, one of the most recurrent forms of the person of peripheral power is the "interim pastor," one who does not *want* the position of permanent pastor. He or she serves as a temporary pastoral leader, worship leader, preacher, and "no strings attached" adviser to the congregation—while they look for a pastor.

You may well say that such a stance of peripheral function is possible only after long tenure in working your way up the totem pole of prestige. You may be right. But I think it comes from something more than just climbing a bureaucratic ladder. I am confident that the prize of freedom in relation to power comes from intentionally forming deep relationships to people on a face-to-face basis—"mid good report and evil report"—over however many or few years it may take. It comes from *steadfastness* of trust-based relationships when the going gets rough. It comes from "taking a stand with the pieces" in transient conflicts between people and within institutions until a true healing takes place. This takes patience and stubbornness to stick with some very difficult situations. More than that, it takes a sense of humor that sees the absurd in most of the things people carry as grudges all their lives. At base it calls for being angry appropriately when provoked to wrath, but being quick to reconcile before the sun goes down on your wrath. Finally, it calls for being kind and tenderhearted to one another, and forgiving one another as God for Christ's sake forgave us. Just such an attitude has a humorous side effect. If your adversaries think they can get rid of you permanently, they are likely to do so. However, if they find out that they have to live with you, they are more likely to find a way of peace.

The Prize of Ministry to the "Broken Ones"

Many years ago, amid the wreckage of a severe institutional conflict of personalities, I was asked: "Where do you stand in all of this?" My reply was: "With the pieces." One of the prizes "of the upward call of God in Christ Jesus" (Phil. 3:14) is my privilege and yours to take a stand with the pieces of human hearts in shattered covenants, hopes, and relationships. In my own life the struggle to be free, to find an integrity of my own being in the middle of the brokenness of my family and community, has been a work of equipping myself to minister to the broken ones.

Such a ministry calls for a capacity to see through one's own tears and beyond the tears of others to find fresh new alternatives to futility. It calls for an ingenuity to find a new design and organization in the disarray of the pieces of people's lives.

Our son Bill gave me a parable for the ministry to broken lives in an event that happened to him when he was five. I brought him a little balsa-wood airplane. The propeller was driven by a long, strong rubber band which, when twisted and allowed to unwind, would turn the propeller and cause the plane to fly. Bill enjoyed this toy out of doors, but one evening he was flying it in the basement. He let it go and it smashed to pieces against the wall. He cried profusely, and I went to him from upstairs to see what was wrong. By the time I reached him, he had ceased to cry and a grin of discovery was on his face. He said: "Daddy, I smashed my plane, but I know what I can do about it. I can make me a slingshot out of that big rubber band." Human heartbreak is painful; discovery of how to rebound with a creative alternative for the pieces of broken dreams is the exercise of freedom that leads to consolation and from there to the joy of creativity.

We must "sit with" the depressed person, listen with empathy, and even give medical attention for the ravages of the depression upon his or her body. As we do these things, we find that the depressed person can see only *one* way out of his or her pain. It may be to quit a job, to break up a marriage, to "go limp" in total helplessness and be a mental patient the rest of his or her life, or, at worst, to commit suicide. All the while, the pastoral counselor, the family members, and the physician are trying to inspire the person to consider at least one or two, and maybe three, ways of putting life back together again.

Another parable comes to me from our son Bill when he was about six years old. After he was all through taking his bath one evening, he was diligently working with the drain device. I asked him what he was doing. He replied: "Daddy, I have figured out *sixteen* ways to fix this thing if it gets broken." One way was not enough! He had to have fifteen more.

Getting closed up to *one* solution for a problem brings you and me to despair when that one approach fails. The capacity to generate fresh alternatives is a perennial power toward freedom within the limits of our habitation. One of the refreshing prizes of my years of struggle to be free is to engage in what Jürgen Moltmann calls "the experiment hope" with grief-stricken, brokenhearted, and depressed persons whom I encourage and inspire to figure out "sixteen ways" of repairing the damage to their lives. The psalmist expressed it best:

> Fill me with joy and gladness;
>   let the bones which thou hast broken rejoice. . . .
> The sacrifice acceptable to God is a broken spirit;
>   a broken and contrite heart, O God, thou wilt not
>   despise.   (Ps. 51:8, 17)

Of all the "sixteen ways to fix this thing if it is broken," making a sacrifice of the broken spirit to God is the first move toward wholeness. The unmixed joy of being a pastor to people in this "experiment hope" offsets and neutralizes the perplexities and ambiguities that attend the task when our own tragic sense of life would otherwise overcome me. This unmixed joy is one of the prizes of the struggle to be free.

The Prize of Sharing the Weight of the Tragic Sense of Life

I have spent the last eight years of my life working in a large inner-city charity hospital, the central teaching hospital of the University of Louisville School of Medicine. It is a trauma emergency center; residents and medical students in their junior and senior years are the first line of service to people with "all manner of diseases." Raw green recruits they are, and they are accompanied by equally green theological students who are equally scared. The years of my own struggle to be free seem to have created for me an ambience that makes it easy for these physicians and pastors in the making to share with me the weight of their own tragic sense of life. As they fight delaying actions and often losing battles for the lives of cardiac patients and victims of collisions, gunshot wounds, suicidal overdoses, and stubbornly unresponsive psychotic deterioration of personality, I see them throw their whole energies into the battle.

When our son Charles was a third-year student at the School of Medicine where I teach, he lost a patient for whom he and his team of medical students were caring. She was a woman in her thirties, the mother of two children, and a widow. Charles and his colleagues had come to respect her very much. They went home one evening thinking she was well on the way to recovery, but that night she died suddenly. When he came to work and learned that she had suddenly died, he was overwhelmed with grief. He felt that he had not been the kind of doctor he should have been. He said: "I don't think I would want me for a physician."

I said that he was a physician in the making and should not carry the whole burden of blame. A streptococcus infection had apparently taken her life. A few days later, as I was leaving the city, I called him to tell him where I was going and said to him: "Your brother went to Vietnam and that was his hell on earth to go through. Now I guess this is your hell to go through. I'll go through it with you, too." He said: "No, Dad, I don't think we are going *through* hell. We are just getting accustomed to the heat." Then I said: "Harry Truman said that if we can't stand the heat, we should get out of the kitchen." Then Charles's humor took over. He said: "Dad, I *think* Teddy Roosevelt said that first." We laughed, and I said: "When we get the time, we will have to research that one."

The discipline of caring for others has its casualties. Yet we exercise our freedom by descending into hell with the good news of health and hope. "Hell" here is not a lightly used swear word; it is the experience of grappling with the issues of life and death. The gates of hell cannot hold out against someone who does this in the name of the crucified and risen Christ. To me, one of the prizes of my struggle to be free is to have the privilege of descending into the nethermost regions of the human spirit with my colleagues in these dire and crucial human situations. Had I not been ushered into the freedom for which Christ has set us free, I would not be able to do so.

The Prize of Dreaming
with Young Persons of Vision

Finally, one of the most renewing prizes of my struggle to be free is the opportunity of dreaming dreams with young persons who have visions. I know that very early in life we can become enchanted with what someone has called "the habitual vision of greatness." I never lack for a steady stream of young persons who have a vision of what they want to become that is greater than what they are now. The level of their aspirations is attainable, but not without a struggle with those forces that would keep them from reaching their goal. And they may not be able to reach that level of aspiration without encouragement from some veteran who has not forgotten the visions of his or her own youth. They need the encouragement of someone who has to a reasonable degree fulfilled those aspirations but is not without dreams, in the still of the night, of what the struggle was like. Hence, you or I become mentors even as we were given mentors by God; we become facilitators, even as some of God's most unlikely servants ran interference for us when we struck opposition and smoothed the way for us when the going was roughest.

The most poignant aspect of the prize of dreaming with young persons is to see those whose lives have been so blighted by disease and disaster that high aspirations no longer seem to exist. What they have left is fantasies that occasionally break through into words and escape more rapidly than they appeared and do not return. I sit with and hurt with and for these too. My time is not wasted. Yet I come away filled with sadness for those with visions snuffed out, angry that their jaws have been lowered, their eyes glazed, and their bodily movements thrown into slow motion, even sometimes before they were out of their teens or far into their twenties.

These are, thank God, the exceptions and not the rule. Hope and joy come with those who have stacks of poems they have written; portfolios of art they want me to see; a song with lyrics and music blended; a plan for a book that has not been written before, insofar as we can discover; a project for starting a new kind of ministry of the gospel to a particular group of people whose sufferings have isolated them from the mainstreams of life. Here they come! No one organized their coming; no special package was prepared for the crowds like them. There is no crowd like them! Their visions are like solitaire diamonds in settings all their own.

We sit together in my office, or in my study at home, or at a lunch table in a crowded cafeteria at the hospital, or in their hospital rooms where they are patients, or at a convention where we "connect back up" after years of not seeing each other daily. I ask: "Will you catch me up on what you are into these days? What new things are you seeing?" The time flies and I forget about anything but what they are telling me. They punch my memory for associations as if it were a computer. My mind prints out past thoughts, new associations, bibliographies, and names of people who also can share their visions. Suddenly we are propelled out of the gravity of the particular world in which we started. Drawn into a new realm of being, we are orbiting to the music of the spheres of new thought. Then I return to my meditations at home after our conference is over and thank God that the prophet Joel's words, quoted by Peter at Pentecost, have come true:

> And in the last days it shall be, God declares,
> that I will pour out my Spirit upon all flesh,
> and your sons and your daughters shall prophesy,
> and your young men shall see visions,
> and your old men shall dream dreams.   (Acts 2:17)

What prizes of the struggle to be free!

Epilogue

I HAVE AFFIRMED that to live creatively is to struggle to be free. Yet to be free lays upon you and me the responsibility and the discipline that inhere in the freedom that comes to us. To accept that responsibility and that discipline creates a zone of joy in our existence. We then fulfill the chief end of our existence, which is to glorify God and to enjoy God's love and presence. Not to accept that disciplined responsibility is to lose our own sense of integrity and our awareness of fellowship with God.

The end result of the freedom within responsible discipline is the rediscovery of a certain playfulness of being, a certain childlikeness—quite another thing than childishness. The latter has been put away in behalf of maturity. Yet that maturity, with all its awareness of finitude and limitation, has a playfulness that defies limits. As William Blake says in his *Auguries of Innocence,* the rediscovered playfulness enables you and me

> To see a world in a grain of sand
> And a heaven in a wild flower,
> Hold infinity in the palm of your hand
> And eternity in an hour.

This kind of vision seems to be a given grace of the little children like whom Jesus told us we must become if we are to enter the Kingdom of Heaven. I used to wonder what Browning meant when he spoke of "the last of life, for which the first was made." I do not know what it meant to Browning, unless he meant for each reader to do as I am doing—supply his or her own meaning. Until recently I could not do that. Now it seems to me that the childlikeness of which Jesus spoke is a "given" in childhood but is the father of the results of a lifelong struggle to be free in adulthood. As Erik Erikson puts it: "For the pre-senile years, with all of their unavoidable *despair* and disgust, I have posited a strength which is directly perceived by children; wherefore old people and children have an affinity for each other." Hence he adjures us to avoid the unwise pretense of being wise, which he calls "sapientism" (*Toys and Reasons: Stages in the Ritualization of Experience*, p. 114; W. W. Norton & Co., 1977).

The years of later maturity for me, then, I pray, will be years of magic laughter at the multitude of things, behaviors of other people, and tides of human politics that are beyond our control, and of canny alertness to those situations which, with a little bit of luck and a massive demonstration of Providence, we can actually do something about.

In between these extremes may we recapture something of the sense of childlikeness which Selma H. Fraiberg calls "the magic years." I was playing with our four-year-old grandson, Will, the other day. He loves to use our king-size bed as a trampoline. This time his feet were dirty, and I asked him to let me first wash his feet. Then he could jump on the bed.

I took a warm and wet washcloth and washed his feet. Then I took the cloth to the bathroom to wash the dirt out of it. When I returned, Will was gone. I assumed he had gone out of the bedroom. Hence, I went about hanging a suit up and placing some shoes in the closet.

Suddenly he jumped from behind the bed where he had been hiding. I reacted with great surprise, saying: "Where on earth did you come from, and how did you get in this room?" He said: "I came through that wall right there!" I said: "Well, I don't see any hole in the wall." He said: "I know. I fixed it back just like it was and painted it this color," pointing to a special color in the wallpaper. "And," he said, "if you will touch it with your finger, you will see that it's still wet paint." I reached and touched it with my finger and looked at my finger and said: "My goodness! You're right! It *is* still wet!" At which point both of us broke into hilarious laughter together. What fun! What magic!

It may well be that the joyful meeting of children and older persons in the magic years of imagination and shared freedom is the secret that enables some older persons to take a fresh new growth and spontaneous renewal without which many others decide that life is over, fold up, and die. I am persuaded that there is a biochemistry present in our body that corresponds with the laughter my grandson and I share. Whether there is or not, I know that his and my laughter made me *want* to live for many years to come. Life seems only to have begun in the ecstasy of such an event.